Teaching Storytelling in Classrooms and Communities

Unleash the transformative power of storytelling to build belonging, ignite critical consciousness, and amplify students' voices. This dynamic book equips educators who work with middle and high school aged youth to teach storytelling in their classrooms or community organizations.

Through inspiring examples and hands-on teaching strategies, the authors show you how to build trust and foster community, explore diverse storytelling modes and formats, guide students in developing effective and ethical social impact stories, and more. You'll also discover practical tools to help students broaden their story's reach and impact through collaboration and coalition building. Each chapter brims with student examples, ready-to-use teaching tips, and experiential activities, plus questions designed to spark dialogue and help students awaken and embrace the storyteller within. There are also reflective prompts to support your own journey as both a facilitator and participant in the storytelling exchange.

Packed with practical resources, moving narratives, and actionable tips, this book is your essential guide to cultivating a supportive learning community, increasing student engagement, and unlocking young people's leadership potential through the vehicle of storytelling.

Maru Gonzalez, EdD, is an Associate Professor, University Faculty Scholar, and Youth Development Specialist in the Department of Agricultural and Human Sciences at North Carolina State University. She serves as co-director of #PassTheMicYouth, a multimedia program aimed at amplifying youth voices and providing practitioners with research-based resources for teaching social impact storytelling.

Michael Kokozos, PhD, is an Associate Director of Teaching and Learning at the University of Pennsylvania. In addition to his role at Penn, he serves as a curriculum consultant for North Carolina State University and as an instructor for Global Online Academy. With over two decades of experience across K-12 and higher education, he is dedicated to fostering global citizenship, community engagement, and belonging.

Christy M. Byrd, PhD, is an Associate Professor in the Department of Teacher Education and Learning Sciences at North Carolina State University who uses her research and outreach to help young people tell stories that raise awareness and inspire positive change in their communities.

"*Teaching Storytelling in Classrooms and Communities* offers a needed focus on the power of story for youth development, voice, and activism. The book's practical tips and engagement strategies will be a terrific resource for classroom teachers and community educators."

Ben Kirshner, PhD, *Author of* Youth Activism in an Era of Education Inequality

"Gonzalez, Kokozos, and Byrd have written a wonderful and comprehensive guide for those seeking to center youth while collaboratively building culturally relevant classrooms and communities. They remind us of the future we can build right now for equity and justice in learning environments."

Anneliese Singh, PhD, LPC, *Professor of Social Work and Associate Provost for Faculty Development and Diversity/Chief Diversity Officer, Tulane University and Author of* The Racial Healing Handbook

"*Teaching Storytelling in Classrooms and Communities* offers an amazing resource for youth workers and classroom educators who are committed to actively supporting the transformative power of youth voices, personal storytelling, meaningful and critical dialogue, agency, and activism. Si se puede, con apoyo!

Ximena Zúñiga, PhD, *Co-Editor of* Intergroup Dialogue: Engaging Difference, Social Identities and Social Justice *(Routledge)*, Dialogues Across Difference *(Russell Sage Foundation), and* Readings for Diversity and Social Justice *(Routledge)*

"*Teaching Storytelling in Classrooms and Communities* gives life to the good and necessary work that is capable of creating transformational counter-narratives to foster critical engagement in youth. It pushes them to think about their identities, communities, and power, while arming them and their teachers with foundational knowledge, skills, and dispositions necessary to help create change. It adeptly and beautifully provides both a theoretical and practical exploration of how to foster meaningful action.

I will use *Teaching Storytelling in Classrooms and Communities* as a roadmap for supporting my students in using their voices as a vehicle for empowerment and change. For providing students and educators with the terminology, contexts, and the know-how to prepare young people to fight for the world they deserve, this invaluable text should be in the library of every educator committed to the cause of a more just and joyful world."

Sam Texeira, *Chicago Public Schools, Teachers for Social Justice, 2019 Boston Public Schools Educator of the Year, 2014 Donovan Urban Teaching Scholar, Black Teacher Project Cohort III*

"This book is a fantastic resource for educators committed to amplifying student voices, increasing student engagement, and building connection and belonging. With extensive experience working with youth, the authors provide a practical guide to teaching storytelling through a variety of mediums in the classroom and beyond. If you have ever wondered how to inspire students to create awareness and inspire action for social change, this book is an essential resource for developing empathetic movers and shakers of the next generation."

Crystal Chen Lee, Ed.D, *Associate Professor, English Education, North Carolina State University, Co-Author of* Amplifying Youth Voices through Critical Literacy and Positive Youth Development: The Potential of University-Community Partnerships

"Teaching Storytelling in Classrooms and Communities is a great resource for those working to empower the next generation of change makers. When youth learn how to utilize effective and ethical approaches to storytelling, they unlock the potential to move others with their stories and improve their communities and their world. This resource is full of engaging, inclusive, and comprehensive content that will support any educator in their work to lift up, activate, and amplify youth voices."

Carlos Moses, *4-H Youth Development Coordinator*

"Unlock the transformative power of storytelling with *Teaching Storytelling in Classrooms and Communities: Amplifying Student Voices and Inspiring Social Change*. This compelling guide empowers educators to foster student competence and confidence through practical strategies and insightful examples. Maru Gonzalez and the authors illustrate how storytelling is a dynamic tool for driving ethical social change, and show us how to utilize this tool to the fullest in our classrooms, laboratories, and lives. Perfect for educators committed to creating inclusive and impactful learning environments, this book is your essential resource for inspiring the next generation of critical thinkers and empathetic leaders."

Michelle Jewell, *Communications and Engagement Manager for the Southeast Climate Adaptation Science Center & President of the Science Communicators of North Carolina*

"Gonzalez, Kokozos, and Byrd have written a hopeful, uplifting, and much-needed book that shows us what it really means to center the power of youth storytelling in teaching and learning – to nurture more humane classrooms and to awaken and inspire social change."

Jessica Whitehlaw, PhD, *Adjunct Assistant Professor, University of Pennsylvania Graduate School of Education, Author of* Arts-Based Teaching and Learning in the Literacy Classroom: Cultivating a Critical Aesthetic Practice

Equity and Social Justice in Education Series

Paul C. Gorski, Series Editor

Routledge's Equity and Social Justice in Education series is a publishing home for books that apply critical and transformative equity and social justice theories to the work of on-the-ground educators. Books in the series describe meaningful solutions to the racism, white supremacy, economic injustice, sexism, heterosexism, transphobia, ableism, neoliberalism, and other oppressive conditions that pervade schools and school districts.

Case Studies on Diversity and Social Justice Education, Third Edition
Paul C. Gorski and Seema G. Pothini

Becoming an Everyday Changemaker: Healing and Justice at School
Alex Shevrin Venet

Embracing the Exceptions: Meeting the Needs of Neurodivergent Students of Color
JPB Gerald

Identity-Conscious Practice in Action: Shaping Equitable Schools and Classrooms
Liza Talusan

Social Studies for a Better World, Second Edition: An Anti-Oppressive Approach for Elementary Educators
Noreen Naseem Rodríguez and Katy Swalwell

Teaching Storytelling in Classrooms and Communities: Amplifying Student Voices and Inspiring Social Change
Maru Gonzalez, Michael Kokozos, and Christy M. Byrd

Igniting Real Change for Multilingual Learners: Equity and Advocacy in Action
Carly Spina

Teaching Storytelling in Classrooms and Communities
Amplifying Student Voices and Inspiring Social Change

Maru Gonzalez, Michael Kokozos,
and Christy M. Byrd

NEW YORK AND LONDON

Designed cover image: © Aditi Rao

First published 2025
by Routledge
605 Third Avenue, New York, NY 10158

and by Routledge
4 Park Square, Milton Park, Abingdon, Oxon, OX14 4RN

Routledge is an imprint of the Taylor & Francis Group, an informa business

© 2025 Maru Gonzalez, Michael Kokozos, Christy M. Byrd

The right of Maru Gonzalez, Michael Kokozos, Christy M. Byrd to be identified as authors of this work has been asserted in accordance with sections 77 and 78 of the Copyright, Designs and Patents Act 1988.

All rights reserved. No part of this book may be reprinted or reproduced or utilized in any form or by any electronic, mechanical, or other means, now known or hereafter invented, including photocopying and recording, or in any information storage or retrieval system, without permission in writing from the publishers.

Trademark notice: Product or corporate names may be trademarks or registered trademarks, and are used only for identification and explanation without intent to infringe.

Library of Congress Cataloging-in-Publication Data
Names: Gonzalez, Maru, author. | Kokozos, Michael, author. | Byrd, Christy M., author.
Title: Teaching storytelling in classrooms and communities : amplifying student voices and inspiring social change / Maru Gonzalez, Michael Kokozos, Christy M. Byrd.
Description: New York, NY : Routledge, 2025. | Series: Equity and social justice in education series | Includes bibliographical references.
Identifiers: LCCN 2024057652 (print) | LCCN 2024057653 (ebook) | ISBN 9781032598925 (paperback) | ISBN 9781003461753 (ebook)
Subjects: LCSH: Storytelling. | Middle school students. | High school students.
Classification: LCC LB1042 .G545 2025 (print) | LCC LB1042 (ebook) | DDC 372.67/7044—dc23/eng/20250326
LC record available at https://lccn.loc.gov/2024057652
LC ebook record available at https://lccn.loc.gov/2024057653

ISBN: 978-1-032-59892-5 (pbk)
ISBN: 978-1-003-46175-3 (ebk)

DOI: 10.4324/9781003461753

Typeset in Palatino
by codeMantra

To the youth whose stories

open hearts,
broaden perspectives,
and plant the seeds for a more equitable future.

And to those whose stories are waiting to be told.

Note from the authors: In the preparation of this book, some contributors used AI-based tools, specifically OpenAI's ChatGPT, for assistance with idea generation, drafting, and revising content. This tool was used to help refine and organize sections of the text, provide feedback on phrasing, and offer suggestions for clarifying complex ideas. We have ensured that all content is original or properly credited and take full responsibility for the validity and integrity of the final material. All final decisions on the content, structure, and conclusions were our own.

Contents

Foreword xiii
Meet the Authors xvi
Acknowledgements xviii
Preface xx

Introduction 1

1 Storytelling and Social Change 13

2 Trust, Community, and Connection: Laying the Groundwork for Authentic Storytelling 35

3 Ready, Set, Warm-Up: Activities for Awakening the Storyteller Within 61

4 From Spoken Word to Photography: Exploring Storytelling Formats 73

5 Positionality, Power, and Privilege: Building Critical Reflection 94

6 Centering Youth in Social Change Narratives 114

7 The Ethics of Storytelling 134

8 The Story of Me: Nurturing Personal Storytelling 151

9 Exploring Dominant Narratives and Counterstories . . . 173

10 Idea to Impact: Additional Practices for Effective Storytelling 189

11 Beyond the Story: Moving from Awareness to Critical Action 197

Afterword 219

Foreword

As a visually impaired pre-teen, going into middle school was tough. Along with the stress that comes along with transitioning, middle school brought many different questions about my visual impairment from peers, some curious and some ignorant. I wasn't sure how to explain the needlessly complicated subject of visual impairment. I guess the universe heard my thoughts because a week later, our family came across a newsletter informing us about a regional speaking opportunity for a TEDxYouth event—organized by two of this book's authors—with the theme, "From here to everywhere," exploring how local ideas and actions can resonate globally. As soon as I saw this I knew that I wanted to address the topic I had been contemplating, and so I came up with a title (Vision for an Equitable World) and submitted the application.

A few weeks later when I received an email that my application was accepted, I was ecstatic!!! But my first thought was how could I condense the multitude of challenges that visually impaired people face into ten minutes? As I began this journey, I realized that the stage could be a platform not only for sharing my own challenges but also for amplifying the experiences of other visually impaired individuals on their unique journey. I sought wisdom from legally blind adults on their challenges in navigating a sight-centric world. With the guidance of my coach and mentors, I chiseled my talk using the data and information I collected, including those based on my personal experience, to come up with challenges and solutions that covered many aspects of life for visually impaired adults and kids alike.

And so the time came and I presented my TEDx talk and while I could tell that it made an impact on the people around me at the moment, I had no idea what an impact it would make afterwards. Following the official release of my TEDx talk on

YouTube, teachers in my school played it in their classrooms. This sparked engaging conversations among my peers, leading to increased empathy and awareness among both sighted students and educators about how to support visually impaired students. Witnessing the impact of these conversations, my principal shared the talk with the school district superintendent, aiming to extend its reach across the entire school system. The talk has also been featured in the newsletter of Perkins School of the Blind—Paths to Technology. Beyond the education sphere, the talk has grabbed the attention of corporate leaders. They shared the talk on their social media feed and it has also been featured in the Accessibility Employee Resource Group Newsletters of corporates. As my next steps, I plan to collaborate with my local school board to implement digital accessibility in all school materials. I also intend to meet with the town council to discuss the planning of safe and accessible public transportation in our town.

Having stood on the TEDx stage, I've witnessed a profound personal transformation—from battling inner struggles to sharing a vision for societal change and taking steps to realize that vision. The catalyst was the power of the story and the stage. Having the tools and platform to share my story has deepened my confidence in my capacity to inspire change.

Today, I have the privilege of introducing a book, *Teaching Storytelling in Classrooms and Communities: Amplifying Student Voices and Inspiring Social Change,* by authors who have provided me and many other young people the platform to tell our stories. To the authors of this remarkable book: Your dedication to providing opportunities for youth to make an impact on society through their stories is commendable. I strongly suggest this book for all educators, who hold the keys to unlocking curiosity, empathy, and critical thinking in students through the vehicle of storytelling. Within its pages, the book delves into how storytelling has been a catalyst for societal transformation throughout history. It introduces foundational concepts and a framework for social justice, nurturing storytelling through the use of different mediums and within diverse and complex contexts. Most importantly, it emphasizes ethical storytelling, critical analysis,

and representation, and places youth at the heart of narratives that drive social change.

As I read this book, I imagined classrooms and communities buzzing with excitement, where students feel connected, valued, and visible; where they are armed with the tools to develop narratives that transport them beyond facts, figures, and textbooks. They become storytellers themselves with a vision of the world they would like to create, supported by educators, like you, who believe deeply in their promise and potential to build a more compassionate, just, and equitable future. With this book as a guide, I am confident that your students will be transformed, as I have been, by the power of storytelling.

With gratitude and best wishes,
Aditi Rao,
6th grade student, storyteller, and accessibility advocate

Scan the below QR code to listen to Aditi's TEDx Talk

Aditi Rao is a multi-faceted middle schooler with accomplishments in STEM, music, and art. Her singing captivates audiences and her digital art tells powerful stories. As a visually impaired TEDx speaker, she fearlessly shared her personal story and vision for an equitable world. With a passion for social justice, her legal blindness brings a unique drive to champion changes for an equitable world.

Meet the Authors

Maru Gonzalez, EdD, is an Associate Professor, University Faculty Scholar, and Youth Development Specialist in the Department of Agricultural and Human Sciences at North Carolina State University. Her areas of inquiry and outreach include youth development with a focus on storytelling, community engagement, and belonging. Dr. Gonzalez serves as co-director of #PassTheMicYouth, a multimedia program aimed at amplifying youth voices and providing practitioners with research-based resources for teaching social impact storytelling. She has over 20 years of experience working with youth in various capacities across the US, Spain, and Latin America, including as an educator, scholar, intergroup dialogue facilitator, mentor, and school counselor.

Michael Kokozos, PhD, is an Associate Director of Teaching & Learning at the University of Pennsylvania, a curriculum consultant for North Carolina State University and an instructor for Global Online Academy. He is passionate about fostering inclusive learning environments and empowering students through storytelling, with a particular focus on using children's book writing as a tool for promoting social change. His current research focuses on fostering belonging and community within educational settings.

Christy M. Byrd, PhD, is an Associate Professor in the Department of Teacher Education and Learning Sciences at North Carolina State University. Her research examines how students make sense of race and culture in their school environments and shows that inclusive educational environments can bolster motivation, a sense of belonging, and critical consciousness. In her outreach, she helps young people tell stories that raise awareness and inspire positive change in their communities.

Acknowledgements

The process of writing this book was truly a team effort. We are immensely appreciative to all of those whose encouragement, feedback, and support helped us see this project through.

First and foremost, we are forever grateful to Paul Gorski, whose belief in us made this book possible. His feedback—informed by decades of experience and an unwavering commitment to equity and justice—stretched us as educators, advocates, and storytellers, pushing us to dig deep and write to our fullest potential. Lauren Davis has been equally instrumental in guiding our vision for this book from start to finish with encouragement, grace, and an abundance of helpful suggestions.

We extend our deepest appreciation to Dr. Katie McKee and all the students whose work is woven throughout the pages of this book, powerfully illustrating the brilliance of youth voice. We are especially grateful to Aditi Rao and Austin Laufersweiler for their moving foreword and afterword. Their experiences are a testament to the personal and global impact of youth-led storytelling throughout the lifespan. And to the countless youth whose voices inform and drive our work and whose ideas give us hope for a more equitable world, we thank you; your stories are the lifeblood of this book.

We are also indebted to NC State University and the University of Pennsylvania for valuing and uplifting community engaged scholarship. In particular, funding from NC State University's Office of Outreach and Community Engagement and the Agricultural Foundation supported the research and curricular initiatives that shaped our inspiration for this book.

Above all, we thank our families and close friends for their consistent support, validation, and encouragement. We owe a special debt of gratitude to our children and godchildren, who give new meaning and purpose to our work and who inspire us,

every day, to build the world that every child and young person deserves.

Finally, we are profoundly grateful to you, the educators and youth-serving professionals, for your steadfast commitment to young people and your unflinching belief in their capacity to build a more just and compassionate future. May you one day recognize the full scope of your impact.

Preface

Why do you teach? What keeps you going, even and especially amidst hardship?

As educators ourselves, this question—why do we teach?—is one we revisit regularly to keep our practice intentional, reflective, and grounded in purpose. Our reasons for teaching are vast and multi-faceted. We teach to connect; we teach to heal; we teach to open hearts and minds, including our own; we teach to liberate; we teach to inspire and be inspired; we teach for social transformation, with the knowledge that change is a collaborative effort; it's about "we" and not "I." And ultimately, we teach to learn, with the understanding that learning starts by decentering ourselves and listening. *Really listening*.

As we reflect on our own experiences as young people, we recall the sting of *not* feeling listened to, of having our ideas consistently dismissed by adults. We remember what it was like to be told that we should be seen and not heard, even when the decisions being made directly impacted us. We know how it feels to be called naive, to have our leadership capacity called into question because of our age. These memories have undoubtedly pushed us to be the kinds of adults and educators we needed, and deserved, growing up.

Through this pursuit, we found storytelling, a practice that is fundamentally about centering youth voices and *really listening*. Whether in classrooms or communities, teaching storytelling means passing the mic to young people, giving them the stage, and shining a spotlight on their experiences, perspectives, and ideas. It's about trusting students to lead.

In our collective experience as educators, school counselors, scholars, and youth-serving professionals, we have found that the process of building and sharing informed, critically grounded stories can be transformative, not solely for students, but for the educators who guide them and for the audiences

they reach. That's why we wrote this book—because we believe, deeply and unequivocally, in the power of stories to motivate, heal, and transform. Indeed, our work with youth, from issues of school climate and leadership to racial justice and LGBTQIA+ belonging, is continuously inspired, shaped, and driven by their stories.

Aditi Rao, who you met in the foreword, is a prime example. Her vision for creating more accessible schools and communities for visually impaired people has moved us to be more intentional and reflective about our own work, prompting us to ask: What are *we* doing to center and amplify the voices of visually impaired youth? What should we start doing? How can we work in solidarity with visually impaired people to advocate for accessibility?

Stories, like the one Aditi shared, push all of us to think beyond our own experiences, to step outside the constraints of familiarity, to move from complacency toward action, and to imagine new possibilities.

We hope this book will serve as a roadmap for teaching storytelling in your classroom or community organization. Our intention is that it will also be a reflective tool for exploring and, ultimately, reinvigorating your why.

Introduction

Julia sat in the principal's office. Her eyes darted between the clock and the door. It was her second visit in less than a week. Julia's dad, Mr. Perez, was seated beside her. He always had his daughter's back and this time was no different.

Clock, door. Clock, door. Clo-

The door swung open. "I'm sorry I'm late. I was tied up in another meeting." Mr. Sweeting said, marching in like a one man stampede.

Mr. Sweeting pulled up a chair in front of Julia and her dad. "Hi Julia. Afternoon, Mr. Perez. Thanks for being here. What can I do for y'all?"

"Good afternoon, Mr. Sweeting. I appreciate you taking the time to meet with me again about the school's dress code," Julia started. "I've been pulled out of class three times this month. I've missed more than two hours of instruction. I've been shamed in front of my classmates. How does that serve anyone? I'm asking you to reconsider my proposal to coordinate a student-led committee to draft a new dress code."

"Now Julia," Mr. Sweeting began, "I think it's great that you stand up for what you believe in. You're a fighter; I can see that. But I tell my kids that sometimes when you're going down the road of life and you see a bump in the middle of the road, you have to learn to go around the bump and keep moving forward. Julia, I think it's time for you to move for-."

"I teach my kids a different lesson," Mr. Perez interjected. "I tell them that if they're going down the road of life and they see a bump in the middle of the road, they better get out of the car and try like hell to smooth out that bump so the people behind them will have an easier road to travel."

Fun fact: This is a true story. More importantly, though, this is a story we can all relate to. Indeed, we've all come across these characters in our work as educators and youth-serving professionals.

Julia, the student who advocates, persistently and unabashedly, for the causes she believes in.

Mr. Perez, the supportive adult who helps open the doors that might otherwise remain closed, who knows when to sit back and when to speak up.

Mr. Sweeting, the well-meaning albeit misguided educator or administrator who believes he always knows best, even when he clearly doesn't. The one who claims to support students but never fully trusts them to make the right decisions.

Finally, let's dig into the presenting conflict. On the surface, it appears to be gendered dress codes. Fundamentally, though, this story is about the proverbial bumps in the road, the barriers most of us have been conditioned to ignore—like racism, classism, ableism, sexism, heterosexism, and transgender oppression, among others—that perpetuate inequity in the service of an unjust but familiar status quo.

Teaching storytelling is about giving students, like Julia, the tools to shine a spotlight on these bumps and expose the ways they manifest in schools and communities. It's about encouraging adults, like Mr. Perez and Mr. Sweeting, to trust in young people's capacity to lead. And ultimately, teaching storytelling is about moving all of us, students *and* educators, to collectively smooth out the bumps that reinforce injustice so that the people beside us and behind us will have an easier road to travel.

Embracing the Storyteller Within

Everybody, as the saying goes, has a story. Stories are ubiquitous; they teach us about both the universality and the uniqueness of the human experience. The pervasiveness and relatability of stories fuels curiosity and engagement and nurtures empathy. And while each of us engages in storytelling on a regular basis and in different capacities, most of us, if asked, would likely not describe ourselves as storytellers—at least that's been our experience.

Given our collective scholarly and pedagogical interest in storytelling, we often introduce the concept to a group by asking participants—be they students, educators, or fellow academics—whether they view themselves as storytellers. The vast majority, regardless of age and other social identities, do not. While ostensibly disheartening, this response is not at all surprising once we start to unpack the difference between what storytelling is and what people assume it to be.

Indeed, storytelling is not solely an artistic endeavor designed for the creatively inclined; it can *also* serve as a pathway to mutual understanding and critical reflection, an invitation for engagement and dialogue, a call to action. As the political and ideological divides in our country deepen, storytelling offers us a compass, an opportunity to connect, to learn, and to plant seeds that raise public consciousness and inspire social change. In the classroom and within youth-serving organizations, storytelling can be a powerful pedagogical tool for developing critical consciousness and amplifying students' voices. Stories can take complex issues across disciplines—from the scientific to the historical—and make them relatable.

When employed effectively and ethically, storytelling has been shown to reduce prejudice, improve self-esteem, foster connection between and across social identity groups, and motivate social action (Aldana et al., 2016; Checkoway et al., 2016). For young people—especially youth with marginalized identities, whose voices are all too often silenced or dismissed—stories can also serve as a celebration of their contributions and

the continued promise of their ideas to awaken, inspire, and call the public to action.

Teaching Storytelling in Classrooms and Communities focuses primarily on stories for social change, which we conceptualize as social impact storytelling. It's primarily intended for middle and high school teachers across disciplines, as well as youth-serving professionals, including and especially those who work in 4-H, the creative arts, or in after-school, extracurricular, or camp programs. That said, we've found that anyone, regardless of age, can benefit from the process of building and sharing social impact stories. Indeed, we've integrated many of these activities into our undergraduate and graduate-level courses with much success.

In this theory-informed, practice-grounded, and interactive book, you will learn how to integrate various forms of storytelling into your classroom or community organization while fostering student belonging, engagement, and critical consciousness. Throughout the book, we weave in narratives inspired by our own experiences to show, rather than merely tell, what teaching storytelling looks like in practice. Each chapter includes teaching tips and activity spotlights that you can implement in your classroom or community organization, as well as questions for extended student dialogue to awaken and embrace the storyteller within. We also outline reflective questions to guide you in your own process of self-reflection as both a facilitator and participant in the storytelling exchange.

In this introduction, we'll review the theoretical framework that informed this book, outline our guiding principles for teaching storytelling, and provide a brief overview of each chapter.

Theoretical Approach

Let's start by digging into the theoretical approach that grounds this book, namely the Critical Positive Youth Development (CPYD) framework.

CPYD, which we developed in 2020, bridges critical theory with the Five Cs model of positive youth development (PYD). Just as Julia sought to change the gendered dress code at her school, critical theory aims to understand and address power

structures that create and perpetuate inequity (Friere, 1973; hooks, 1994). Of course, speaking out in the way Julia did was not without risk. Indeed, students are more likely to share their ideas and perspectives if they feel supported by at least one adult (Search Institute, 2018). In the case of Julia, that adult was her dad, Mr. Perez. Similarly, the Five Cs of PYD is a strengths-based model for youth thriving focused on developing certain assets—*competence, confidence, connection, character,* and *caring,* defined in more detail below—that lead to *contribution* or the actions one takes to improve their school or community (Lerner et al., 2005). By merging critical theory with the Five Cs model, the goal of CPYD is to strengthen students' capacity to identify and address inequity in a strengths-based and supportive environment, ultimately driving youth-led social change and community engagement. We illustrate the CPYD framework in Figure 0.1 below.

The Seven Cs of CPYD

The seven Cs of CPYD connect the Five Cs of PYD with two additional Cs, contribution through critical action and critical consciousness, all of which are defined below.

1) **Competence:** The ability to successfully manage school, work, and social interactions and obligations.
2) **Confidence:** One's sense of self-worth.
3) **Connection:** Having meaningful relationships across home and social contexts.
4) **Character:** Personal integrity and adherence to a set of ethics.
5) **Caring:** The practice of empathy and compassion for others.
6) **Contribution through critical action:** Engagement that seeks to address injustice with the aim of creating sustainable, systemic social change.
7) **Critical consciousness:** Characterized by critical reflection, political efficacy, and critical action, this C is woven throughout the CPYD framework.

Conceptual Model of Critical Positive Youth Development

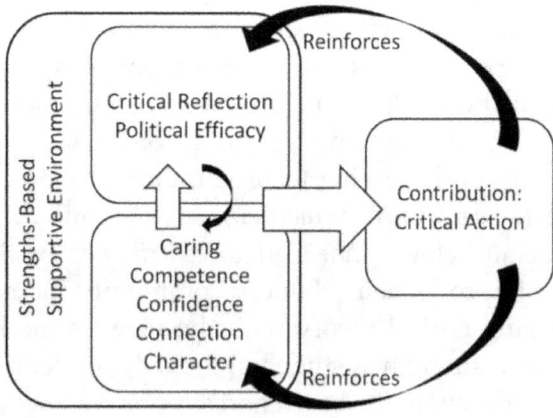

Note: The development of the Five Cs in a strengths-based, supportive environment lays the groundwork for critical reflection and political efficacy. Together, these components lead to the sixth C, contribution through critical action, which reinforces the Five Cs, critical reflection, and political efficacy. Simultaneously, the existence of critical reflection and political efficacy strengthens the Five Cs. The white arrows illustrate conditionality or the presumption that certain conditions must be met before other components can be developed. The black arrows serve as reinforcers. Critical consciousness— consisting of critical reflection, political efficacy, and critical action—is integrated throughout the model and makes up the seventh C of CPYD

FIGURE 0.1 CONCEPTUAL MODEL OF CRITICAL POSITIVE YOUTH DEVELOPMENT
Source: Gonzalez et al. (2020)

Critical Consciousness and CPYD

An educational concept developed by Brazilian pedagogue Paolo Friere (1973), critical consciousness consists of three components: 1) critical reflection, characterized as a critical understanding of power, positionality, and structural inequality; 2) political efficacy or the belief in one's ability to motivate socially just change; and 3) critical action, defined as informed individual or collective action that challenges injustice.

The emphasis on critical consciousness in the CPYD framework is what leads to a version of contribution that is critically informed. Whereas contribution in the Five Cs model might look like volunteering at a soup kitchen, a CPYD framework pushes students to ask questions like: What conditions make soup kitchens necessary in the first place? What can we do,

individually and collectively, to ensure people don't have to rely on soup kitchens to eat?

The tools and strategies highlighted throughout this book and informed by a CPYD framework are meant to assist students in asking questions that expose inequity—just as Julia did—and, ultimately, to build stories that move all of us to contribute to real, sustainable social change.

Guiding Principles for Teaching Storytelling

Our work in teaching storytelling is guided by six overarching principles, which also ground this book.

Space matters. Stories are most valuable when they guide us to new understandings, nurture critical reflection, and transport us to different ways of being and thinking, even when we disagree. Stories are also complex and, often, deeply personal. Asking students to engage in the storytelling exchange, as both a sharer and listener, necessitates a degree of vulnerability that cannot be taken for granted. As educators, we must be intentional about cultivating a culture of mutual respect, trust, and care, and one that actively prioritizes equity, belonging, and wellness. Check out Chapter 2 for strategies on fostering trust, support, and connection in your classroom or community organization.

Story structure is important, so is creativity. A story structure or narrative arc provides students with a framework for telling their story, thus ensuring some degree of intentionality, clarity, and organization. And while we should encourage students to develop a narrative arc, they shouldn't feel constrained by it. Indeed, some students may choose to structure their story in a conventional linear fashion (i.e., beginning, middle, and end) while others may opt to start at the end and work their way backward. Some students may create a story without a clear ending or theme, leaving the audience to reach their own conclusion about the overarching message.

Whatever creative decisions students make in building their story, a clear structure will help them convey their message

more effectively and thoughtfully. Additional information and resources for building a narrative arc can be found throughout the book, including in Chapter 1.

Critical reflection is a prerequisite for students *and* educators. We can't expect students to speak convincingly about social justice issues if they don't understand the conditions that perpetuate injustice (Gorski & Swalwell, 2023). We can't expect them to be intentional and introspective about storytelling if they've never considered the ways in which their social identities and lived experiences inform which stories they tell and how they choose to tell them.

Simultaneously, we cannot effectively teach social impact storytelling if we haven't put in the personal and intellectual work to understand the role of power, equity, and access in our lives and those of our students. Critical reflection is foundational to the work of teaching and building social impact stories. It's woven throughout the pages of this book and we spend Chapter 5 describing it in more detail.

Youth-led stories have and can drive social change. As we detail throughout this book, young people have a long track record of harnessing stories to raise public awareness and mobilize action. If our students are to view themselves as capable of social change—that is, to develop political efficacy—we must make them aware of young people's past and present social justice contributions. Indeed, students will be more likely to share their stories and engage in social change efforts if they view themselves as social change agents whose ideas are worthy of sharing. Simultaneously, *we* are more likely to trust students to lead effectively and meaningfully when we learn to appreciate the full scope of their promise.

Ethics are essential. Ethics are a crucial part of teaching storytelling, especially when students are creating and delivering stories about communities to which they don't belong. An ethical approach to storytelling is characterized by accuracy and transparency, with both the audience and the person(s) whose story students may be sharing. Indeed, ethical storytelling necessitates full and continuous consent of those whose perspectives or experiences are being represented, an acknowledgement of

power dynamics, and a commitment to mitigate potential harm. An emphasis on ethics also necessitates the development of self-reflection and research skills—such as identification of reliable sources, peer review, and fact checking—to ensure students' stories are grounded in truth and authenticity. While ethics is a thread that runs throughout this book, Chapter 7 is dedicated solely to this very important principle.

Stories aren't the end; they're the starting point. Stories are an effective tool for helping students raise awareness about the issues they most care about. When delivered effectively, stories also open the door to dialogue and plant the seeds of social change. But students still have to do the work. Teaching storytelling means positioning stories as the launching pad for collaboration by giving students the resources to broaden the scope of their message—identifying potential partners, pathways, and opportunities to establish community connections and mobilize action. It also means helping students identify where their stories overlap with those of their peers and how they might collaborate to move from awareness to action. Chapter 11 covers how collaboration can expand impact.

Book Overview

Given the focus of this book, we were intentional about sequencing the chapters to scaffold both facilitation and learning. This book is also structured to reflect student learning through the CPYD framework, beginning with a focus on fostering the Five Cs in a strengths-based and supportive environment, moving to critical reflection and political efficacy, and ending with contribution through critical action in the form of storytelling and collaboration.

We begin in Chapter 1, "Storytelling and Social Change," by providing an overview of social impact storytelling, its origins and contemporary applications. In Chapter 2, "Trust, Community, and Connection: Laying the Groundwork for Authentic Storytelling," we review foundational practices for building a culture of care and support, a prerequisite for teaching

storytelling. In Chapter 3, "Ready, Set, Warm-Up: Activities for Awakening the Storyteller Within," we outline low-stakes activities for continuing to foster community while helping students grow more comfortable with the storytelling exchange. In the next chapter, "From Spoken Word to Photography: Exploring Storytelling Formats," we introduce a multitude of mediums for building social impact stories.

Then, we move into Chapter 5, "Positionality, Power, and Privilege: Building Critical Reflection," which digs into the importance of developing a critical understanding of social justice to teach and engage in informed and introspective storytelling for equity and social change. Chapter 6, "Centering Youth in Social Change Narratives," focuses on building student-centered classrooms and community programs that celebrate and amplify the power and promise of youth leadership, past and present. In Chapter 7, "The Ethics of Storytelling," we aim to answer the question "What makes a story ethical?" and provide strategies and activities for teaching ethically grounded storytelling. Chapter 8, "The Story of Me: Nurturing Personal Storytelling," shifts the focus back to individual students by examining the value of critically grounded personal storytelling in a trusting and supportive environment, as well as its role in driving social impact. In Chapter 9, "Exploring Dominant Narratives and Counterstories," we delve into how dominant and counternarratives shape our understanding of ourselves, others, and society and discuss how storytelling can be used to expose, critique, and transform dominant narratives, as well as to amplify, validate, and empower counternarratives.

Following our focus on building students' critical reflection and political efficacy, we shift our focus back to application in Chapter 10, "Idea to Impact: Additional Practices for Effective Storytelling." Specifically, we outline strategies and activities to help guide students through the process of building effective and informed social impact stories. Our last chapter, "Beyond the Story: Moving from Awareness to Critical Action," exemplifies our final guiding principle: *Stories aren't the end; they're the starting point.* This chapter focuses on empowering

students with the knowledge and skills to broaden the scope of their message and drive meaningful social change through collaboration and coalition building. The afterword, written by Austin Laufersweiler, illustrates the ongoing significant impact of youth-led storytelling throughout the lifespan.

Educator Self-Reflection

Because we like to practice what we preach, below is a brief self-reflection activity to complete before jumping into the first chapter.

Hopes and Concerns

Teaching storytelling is fun and exciting but it can also be painful and complex. Jot down what you hope to learn and apply from reading this book. Then, name any concerns you may have and what you need to address them.

Need inspiration? Revisit your hopes and add to them if you think of more along the way!

Hopes

_____

_____

_____

Concerns

_____

_____

_____

References

Aldana, A., Richards-Schuster, K., & Checkoway, B. (2016). Dialogic pedagogy for youth participatory action research: Facilitation of an intergroup empowerment program. *Social Work with Groups, 39*(4), 339–358.

Checkoway, B., Lipa, T., Vivyan, E., & Zurvalec, S. (2016). Engaging suburban students in dialogues on diversity in a segregated metropolitan area. *Education and Urban Society, 48*, 1–15.

Friere, P. (1973). *Education for critical consciousness*. Continuum International Publishing Group.

Gonzalez, M., Kokozos, M., Byrd, C., & McKee, K. (2020). Critical Positive Youth Development: A framework for centering critical consciousness. *Journal of Youth Development, 15*(6). https://doi.org/10.5195/jyd.2020.859

Gorski, P., & Swalwell, K. (2023). *Fix injustice, not kids, and other principles for transformative equity leadership*. ASCD.

hooks, b. (1994). *Teaching to transgress*. Routledge.

Lerner, R. M., Lerner, J. V., Almerigi, J., Theokas, C., Phelps, E., Gestsdóttir, S., Naudeau, S., Jelicic, H., Alberts, A. E., Ma, L., Smith, L. M., Bobek, D. L., Richman-Raphael, D., Simpson, I., Christiansen, E. D., & von Eye, A. (2005). Positive youth development, participation in community youth development programs, and community contributions of fifth-grade adolescents: Findings from the first wave of the 4-H Study of Positive Youth Development. *Journal of Early Adolescence, 25*(1), 17–71.

Search Institute. (2018). *Developmental assets among US youth: 2018 update*. Search Institute.

1
Storytelling and Social Change

Nina stood in front of her school's cafeteria, clutching a piece of folded notebook paper. She looked out into a sea of teachers, took a deep breath, and began to share her story. She spoke of feeling pressure to mask her interests, behaviors, and thought processes to survive in a school that never fully sought to understand or appreciate who she was. She described being the kid no one talked to, the one who spent recess assembling puzzles or laying in the grass, leaning into the firmness of the ground beneath her. She talked about keeping her head down at school, her needs and anxieties hidden, only to lash out at home. She spoke of her adaptability—how she learned to cope when the lights were too bright, when the bell schedule changed without notice, when her classmates were too loud. She described the countless hours spent learning how to make eye contact (but not too much), to ask questions that conveyed interest (but without sounding annoying), to respect personal space (but without seeming withdrawn)—all in an attempt to meet an arbitrary standard of normalcy. "But at what expense?" she asked the audience.

To Nina, "appearing normal" meant not being herself.

And why, Nina wondered, why was *she* the one who always had to adapt to others' needs and expectations instead of the other way around? She didn't need to be fixed; she wasn't broken. What she needed was understanding, openness, flexibility, and grace. She needed the space to show up, and to be embraced, exactly as she was.

As she ended her story, Nina could sense the energy in the room start to shift. Something inside of her was changing too. In that moment, Nina felt the weight of expectations lift. She no longer needed a mask.

Like Nina, agents of social change don't always carry a megaphone or lead a protest march. Most can be found behind the scenes doing the tireless, often thankless, but necessary work that turns moments into movements and—to paraphrase Dr. Martin Luther King Jr.—helps bend the arc of the moral universe toward justice (1968). Indeed, most social change is incremental and invisible, at least initially. Social change often starts by planting seeds of awareness and opening the door to different perspectives and lived experiences, just like Nina did with the teachers at her school. As the late writer and civil rights activist James Baldwin said, "The world changes according to the way people see it, and if you alter even by a millimeter the way people look at reality, then you can change it" (Romano, 1979, para. 55). Social change doesn't have to be big or loud; it isn't always associated with a marked cultural shift or watershed event. Social change *can* and *does* exist in the stories we share—the ones that open hearts and minds, even if only a millimeter at a time.

But how do we teach students to build and share stories that awaken, inspire, and drive meaningful action? Before answering this question, we'll explore the origins of social impact storytelling. We'll also delve into the science of storytelling, review the building blocks of effective social impact stories, and examine the anatomy of a public narrative. Let's get started!

The Origins of Social Impact Storytelling

In our work with young people—whether in classrooms, summer camps, or community-based programs—we are intentional about weaving in narratives, both historical and contemporary, about young people's many contributions to social progress. And we've found that learning these stories can be transformative for students, reinvigorating their belief in the power of their own voices (Gonzalez et al., 2024). As students

work to build and share their own social impact stories, they can also draw inspiration from the many people throughout history and across cultures and contexts who have harnessed the power of narrative to awaken public consciousness and build a more equitable and compassionate world.

So what is storytelling, where did it originate, and what role does it play in driving meaningful social action? Simply put, storytelling is the interactive practice of sharing stories through words, actions, and/or images (De Vos et al., 2003). With roots stemming back thousands of years, storytelling is universal, existing in every country and culture across the globe. Beginning primarily as an oral tradition, storytelling has served a variety of purposes—from preservation of family histories to education and entertainment (Yong, 2017). Storytelling has also been used to inspire local and global social change, particularly in Black and indigenous communities and, increasingly, among young people.

 Teaching Tip:

To scaffold the concept of storytelling, consider engaging students in a free association activity whereby students identify words, phrases, and emotions they associate with storytelling. Their ideas can be used to inform a collective definition of storytelling and foster a broader dialogue about the purpose and origins of this ancient practice.

In the United States, slave narratives unveiled the grim realities of slavery, inspiring and energizing the abolitionist movement (Aje, 2013). In addition to written stories, formerly enslaved people like Frederick Douglas, Sojourner Truth, and William Craft regularly went on tour to share their personal accounts of life in bondage (Greenlee, 2024), undoubtedly leaving an enduring imprint on the American psyche. Musical genres like Bomba, which originated among enslaved Africans in Puerto Rico, provided a way to communicate, express resistance, and coordinate rebellions (Cartagena, 2004).

Among both Black and indigenous populations, oral stories have played a valuable role in knowledge and cultural preservation. For example, indigenous peoples, such as the Blackfoot Tribe in North America, have passed down oral stories to teach life lessons, retain language and physical rituals, and document history, including centuries-old knowledge about the land they inhabit (Starovoitov, 2021). Central to the Blackfoot's oral tradition are creation stories, which hold valuable narrative evidence about the first migration journeys to North America. Restorative practices—grounded in storytelling and aimed at fostering dialogue, connection, and healing—are rooted in indigenous peacemaking (Umbreit et al., 2003).

Examples, both present and past, of young people using stories to mobilize and drive collective action are also numerous and wide-reaching (Kirshner, 2015). Disillusioned by the lack of Black history taught in her school, youth content creator and activist Taylor Cassidy created a social media web series entitled "Fast Black History" to share the untold stories of Black historical figures. Cassidy also harnesses the reach of social media to raise public awareness of racial injustice and amplify the contributions of Black content creators. In the midst of WWII, Sophie Scholl and members of the White Rose—a student-led, non-violent resistance group in Nazi Germany—used a leaflet campaign to tell the story of Jewish persecution and mass murder and call for active resistance (Spitzer, 2020), warning against the perils of apathy and urging fellow citizens to "resist at this last hour as much as he can, aware of his responsibility" (Scholl, 1942). The group's six leaflets spread and multiplied throughout Germany, amassing roughly 15,000 copies.

Historical and contemporary stories—like those of Sophie Scholl, Frederick Douglass, Taylor Cassidy, and others—help us learn from previous injustices so that the world we leave future generations will be better than the one we inherited. Indeed, phrases like "never again" and "never forget," which refer to the Holocaust and other genocides, are a haunting yet necessary reminder that knowing better means doing better. Therein lies the value and promise of social impact storytelling: to raise consciousness and inspire positive, sustainable change while never forgetting the many stories, both told and untold, of those

who came before us and those whose future demands our active commitment to a more equitable world.

The Science of Storytelling: How to Tell an Effective Social Impact Story

A high school student effectively delivers a powerful message about school climate before the school board, ultimately leading to an inclusive and comprehensive anti-bullying and harassment policy. A middle school student uses narrative to educate administrators, classmates, and the local community about building more environmentally sustainable schools. A group of students, recently back from a class trip to Puerto Rico, host a digital photography exhibit to shine a spotlight on the challenges—exacerbated by its colonial status—facing the archipelago and celebrate the power and potential of community-driven action. A couple of youth activists record a podcast episode calling for less school resource officers and increased support staff in schools.

These are among the many youth-led social impact stories that have stuck with us—inspiring, informing, and driving our work with young people. Now it's your turn: Think of a story that has stuck with you. Maybe it struck an emotional chord that had personal resonance. Perhaps the story fundamentally shifted your perspective or pushed you to think about an issue from a different angle, even motivating you to change behavior or take action. What was it about that story that moved you? More broadly, what is it about stories that make us react?

 Teaching Tip:

Ask students to think of a story that has stayed with them. Next, instruct them to identify elements of the story that made a lasting impact. After students share as a large group or in pairs, ask: What makes a story effective? As you move through the various aspects of social impact storytelling, be sure to reinforce students' learning by referring back to their examples and experiences.

We can find the answer to that question in our brains. According to Paul Zak, a professor who studies the neuroscience of human connection, inspiring stories increase the levels of cortisol and oxytocin in our brains, which can ultimately drive behavioral change (2015). In a study by Barraza and Zak (2009), participants were instructed to watch two video clips of a young child with terminal brain cancer interacting with his father. The first video included a dramatic arc and the second did not. The study's results revealed that participants' cortisol and oxytocin levels increased substantially while watching the first video but did not change during their viewing of the second video. Researchers have also found that heightened oxytocin was positively correlated with increased empathy, which subsequently motivated participants to donate money. In another study, researchers found that when heightened oxytocin was coupled with an increase in ACTH, a fast-acting arousal hormone triggered by capturing one's attention, participants were even more likely to donate (Lin et al., 2013).

Dramatic arcs aside, stories that highlight the experiences of individuals can help us understand and feel more connected to an issue and mitigate what Paul Slovic (2007) refers to as psychic numbing, a psychological phenomenon that explains our tendency to become indifferent when confronted with large-scale tragedies or atrocities such as war, famine, and genocide. To build on the above referenced example of the terminally ill boy and his father, let's take the issue of pediatric cancer, which is on the rise with an estimated 400,000 children receiving a diagnosis every year (World Health Organization, 2021). While most of us are not compelled to address, or even think about, a public health concern of that magnitude, we have likely all been moved, at one time or another, to donate to medical fundraising campaigns that narrate the personal perils of pediatric cancer and put a name and face to such a daunting reality.

The science of storytelling indicates that emotional narratives, particularly those that focus on individual experiences and draw and sustain our attention, can motivate action. How can we build on and apply this knowledge—what Zak refers to as "the neuroscience of narrative" (2015)—to help students maximize

the impact of their stories and drive social change? We'll start by focusing on the narrative arc.

Developing a Narrative Arc

Let's revisit one of our guiding principles for teaching storytelling: *Story structure is important, so is creativity*. Indeed, students should be encouraged to outline their story's structure or narrative arc, including a beginning, middle, and an end, though specific sequencing and creative decisions should be left up to each student.

We should also consider that visual modes of storytelling, like photography and visual art, often rely less on a traditional narrative arc to convey a message. When it comes to visual art, for example, students may want audience members to fill in their story's gaps using their own interpretive lens. In other instances, their narrative arc may be clearer. For instance, a student creating a photo essay can intentionally sequence photographs such that their story structure is explicitly communicated. For visual art, students may choose to supplement their story with an artist's statement or corresponding poem to more clearly convey their intended message.

Before we break down specific components of the narrative arc, let's briefly look at the other elements of a story: the characters, the setting, and the conflict. For social impact stories, Niemand (2023) recommends positioning the institutions (e.g., media, government, education, economy) that sustain inequity and reinforce oppression (e.g., racism, sexism, capitalism, ableism) as the setting and conflict the character(s) must confront. As students move through the storybuilding process, ask them to identify their character(s), the setting, and the conflict.

> **Teaching Tip:**
>
> Ethics plays an integral role in storytelling and must be considered when making decisions about how characters are represented, particularly if the story being told is not one's own. Be sure to check out the chapter on ethical storytelling for additional information and guidance.

Now we are ready to zoom back into the narrative arc of a story by exploring its beginning, middle, and end.

- ♦ **Beginning:** When it comes to developing an effective social impact story, the beginning is akin to making a first impression: The first few seconds are crucial and can make or break a student's connection with the audience. Indeed, the beginning of a story presents a valuable opportunity to grab the audience's attention, make clear the problem or conflict, identify the characters and setting, persuade them to feel invested in the issue(s) at hand, and set the tone for the rest of the story.
- ♦ **Middle:** Traditionally, the middle of a story includes rising action whereby a character(s) is faced with a challenge(s) to overcome leading to a climax and falling action. This part of a social impact story is a fitting opportunity to share and substantiate main ideas using accurate, relevant sources from trustworthy authors or publications. See Chapter 7 for tips on how to assist students in assessing the credibility of their sources. If the beginning of a story states the problem, the middle of the story elaborates the *what* and *why* of the problem and introduces potential solutions.
- ♦ **End:** The end of a story wraps up the overarching arc while reemphasizing the main point(s) and proposed solution(s). Often, stories also include a moral or lesson learned. Because the goal of social impact stories is to create awareness that leads to change, students should think about how they can leave a lasting impression. For instance, some may end with a call to action.

Additional story building practices and exercises can be found in Chapters 3 and 10. Details and descriptions of various storytelling formats are available in Chapter 4.

Understanding Social Issues

Building social impact stories requires a fundamental understanding of social justice and social issues. Below are some

suggestions to scaffold these concepts with students and help them think more deeply about social issues they care about.

First thing's first: What is a social issue? A social issue, also known as a social problem, describes social conditions that negatively impact large groups of people (Eagle et al., 2020). Examples of social issues include poverty, homelessness, unemployment, housing discrimination, anti-LGBTQIA+ bullying, health disparities, gender discrimination in the workplace, book bans, environmental racism, and parks and playgrounds that are inaccessible to people with disabilities. Social justice seeks to address social problems by working toward equity and access for all people. Because matters related to environmental justice have societal implications, they are also considered social issues (Solomonian & Di Ruggiero, 2021).

To assess and build upon what students already know, consider facilitating a free association activity in which you ask students to state words, phrases, or examples that come to mind when they hear "social issue(s)." Leveraging students' insights and ideas, work with them to identify similarities between and among the items listed and synthesize those ideas to generate a working definition. Feel free to add your own ideas and examples to deepen understanding, including how social justice and social issues are related.

What social or environmental issue(s) do students care about? Once students understand and can identify social issues, ask them to make a list of social or environmental issues they care about. If they feel comfortable, consider asking students to share their list with a partner, in small groups, or with the class. Encourage students to think about why they care about these issues and how these issues impact them, the people in their school, and the local community.

Next, ask students to choose one issue they would like to focus on, reminding them that social impact stories are often complex and intersectional. For example, a lack of access to healthy food often cuts across racial and class lines, disproportionately impacting communities of color and those living below the poverty line.

How and with whom can students create impact? To answer this question, students should take stock of who they

know, starting with those closest to them. Perhaps they will identify family and close friends as those with whom they can have the greatest impact, followed by members of their school and local community. Students may even include congressional representatives and other elected officials like school board members, especially if their issue has significant community implications. Given the reach of social media, encourage students to think about ways to build connections and raise awareness online. Remind students that identifying *how* and *with whom* they can create impact will help guide the framing of their story with the audience(s) in mind.

Integrating Aristotle's Three Rhetorical Appeals

If you haven't already, ask students to think about a social impact story that has stuck with them, perhaps even shifting their perspective about a given topic. Before beginning, model this activity by sharing your own example(s), as we have, and remind students to adhere to the community agreements for building a respectful and dialogic learning community (see Chapter 2). Instruct students not to share examples that are or may be received as offensive or discriminatory, particularly in reference to someone's identity. For instance, a student sharing a story of people lobbying to ban books with LGBTQIA+ characters from a public library will likely offend many of their peers, including and especially those who are LGBTQIA+. Such an example is also discriminatory and presents an affront to LGBTQIA+ identities.

If time allows, encourage students to share in pairs or small groups. Instruct each student to explain what elements of the story made it effective; each group should take note of themes or patterns that emerge across stories. Students will then report their findings to the class. Drawing on students' examples and experiences, segue into a broader dialogue about persuasive storytelling and Aristotle's three rhetorical appeals (2005), outlined in the box below.

> **Ethos:** An appeal to character, in which the storyteller establishes trust and credibility with the audience. Examples include the use of reliable sources and speaking from firsthand experience.
> **Logos:** An appeal to logic through the use of data, like graphs and statistics, to support a point.
> **Pathos:** An appeal to emotion, whereby the storyteller draws on sentiment and universally shared values to connect with an audience. Examples include personal anecdotes and vivid or inspirational language.

As mentioned previously, a vast and growing body of neurological research has demonstrated that emotional stories heighten empathy, ultimately driving action (Barraza & Zak, 2009; Zak, 2015). Yet while emotion is certainly an effective tool in the storytelling exchange, it should never be used to evoke misguided fear or spread misinformation. For instance, campaigns aimed at banning bathroom access to transgender people have long relied on the myth that trans-inclusive bathroom policies would invite male predators into women's bathrooms, putting young girls at risk of sexual assault. Such a narrative, which is unequivocally false, exploits the public's legitimate fear of sexual assault to generate support for a baseless cause while simultaneously harming trans people, who are disproportionately more likely to be targets—rather than perpetrators—of violence (Murchison et al., 2019).

Ultimately, the use of emotion is a creative and personal decision, often varying by format. Whereas spoken word poetry tends to rely quite heavily on emotion, some storytelling formats, like TEDx style talks, focus more on ideas and solutions than sentiments and personal anecdotes. Also worth noting is that students need not rely solely on sadness or sympathy to employ pathos. Indeed, there exists a myriad of complex human sentiments that students can and should tap into, such as joy,

hope, courage, and frustration. Humor can also be used to appeal to emotion.

How and when to use rhetorical appeals is also dependent on the audience. A story intended for policymakers will likely include more data and less emotion than one geared toward family and friends. Still, students should think about what qualifies *them* to tell a particular story. While they are by no means expected to be content experts, including a personal connection to the issue will go a long way in establishing credibility and appealing to ethos. For example, a young person building a story related to environmental sustainability may highlight the burden young people feel in ultimately having to shoulder the responsibility of previous generations' climate inaction. Such a message appeals to ethos, even if not delivered by an environmental scientist, because it is being communicated by someone with a personal connection to and stake in environmental sustainability.

 Activity Spotlight: Identifying and Applying Ethos, Pathos, and Logos

Below are a couple of recommendations to guide students' learning of these concepts.

1. Show students clips of famous speeches and ask them to identify the use of ethos, pathos, and logos.
2. To move from identification to application, encourage students to engage in role playing. For example, divide students into groups of three, assigning each group a different rhetorical appeal along with a fake product to advertise (e.g., Bob's Cereal, Spring Blossom perfume, etc.). Each group should develop a commercial or magazine advertisement using the rhetorical appeal they have been assigned.

Building Consensus

A significant part of my (i.e., Maru) research and outreach efforts focuses on LGBTQIA+ youth belonging. As part of that work, I regularly facilitate capacity building workshops with a variety of populations, including educators, parents, youth-serving professionals, and faith communities across urban, suburban, and rural communities in the United States and Latin America. I have found that while people's understanding and awareness of LGBTQIA+ youths' needs varies widely, they consistently agree with the notion that all students benefit from a supportive and caring environment. Regardless of political or religious affiliation, this belief is the common ground we all share and it's an entry point through which I engage in dialogue about what it means to support, affirm, and include LGBTQIA+ youth.

In today's divisive political climate, finding common ground when conveying a message to a broad audience with wide-ranging beliefs is not just possible, it's necessary. Learning how to identify and highlight shared values and goals, as illustrated in Figure 1.1, will assist students in generating the support needed to move ideas forward.

FIGURE 1.1 COMMON GROUND VENN DIAGRAM

Below are three strategies for helping students find common ground and build consensus when delivering their story to the

general public and/or people who may not initially share their perspective:

1. **Consider message framing.** When building a social impact story, we make decisions about what content to include, what to leave out, and *how* to convey information. These decisions, which impact the extent to which a story is persuasive, describe a phenomenon known as message framing (Kühberger, 1998). The frames we create for an audience can impact how they perceive and feel about an issue and, ultimately, what they do in response (Kendall-Taylor & Gibbons, 2018).

Among educators and youth-serving professionals, framing our perception of young people from a strengths-based rather than a deficit perspective helps us focus on and nurture students' assets (Search Institute, 2018) rather than viewing them as problems to be solved. Similarly, reframing language related to educational outcomes among students—such as using "opportunity gap" rather than "achievement gap"—takes into account that student performance is not solely determined by intellect but rather the resources and opportunities that support their success, which not all young people have access to in equal measure (Shulka et al., 2022).

Message framing is also frequently used in social and political campaigns. For example, reframing the issue of "gun control" to one of "gun safety" has helped shift the narrative from government control of personal liberties to a more unifying message that emphasizes public health and responsible gun ownership.

The impact of frames was powerfully displayed in a segment for Jimmy Kimmel Live in which reporters asked passersby whether they preferred Obamacare or the Affordable Care Act (Porter, 2013). Unaware that Obamacare and the Affordable Care Act refer to the same federal statute, the vast majority pledged allegiance to the Affordable Care Act, with one ironically claiming "the name says it all." As participant responses in the segment made clear, the public relies on frames to help guide

their decisions, especially when they lack information about issues. In this case, the individuals interviewed bought into the negative frames and media narratives about Obamacare, despite agreeing with most, if not all, of its provisions.

Even changing how a question is asked can shift the public's opinion on an issue. Case in point: In 2010, a CBS/*New York Times* poll found that 70% of Americans supported gays and lesbians serving openly in the US military (Hechtkopf). When the wording of the same question changed from "gays and lesbians" to "homosexuals," support dropped from 70% to 59%. This 11% difference—while troubling—should not be surprising, especially when we understand the historical framing of "homosexual" as a term used to connote pathology and advance harmful measures against gay, lesbian, bisexual, and queer people (Katz, 1995).

2. **Focus on the movable middle.** When it comes to most social and environmental issues, public opinion tends to fall along a spectrum. On one side are those who strongly agree with a given issue while the other end is occupied by those in stark opposition. When championing a cause, most of us tend to focus solely on one extreme of the continuum: either futilely seeking understanding from those with whom we will never agree or preaching to the choir. And while sometimes the choir is in need of practice, building consensus is about telling stories that reach a broad audience—those that focus on a unifying idea and steer clear of partisan rhetoric. The space that exists between strong agreement and fierce opposition is known as the movable middle and is illustrated in Figure 1.2.

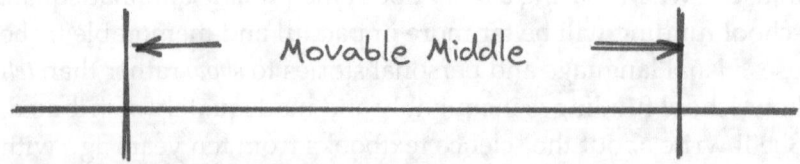

FIGURE 1.2 MOVABLE MIDDLE VISUALIZATION

Creating a story that resonates with this group—those who are open to listening and learning yet who hold varying and nuanced perspectives—yields greater possibilities for broad change. During the COVID-19 pandemic, public health officials combatted vaccine hesitancy by tailoring their message to those in the movable middle, the millions of Americans who fell somewhere between staunch vaccine refusal and acceptance of all vaccines (Sauer & Limaye, 2021). By building trust through effective and consistent messaging, physicians and public health experts successfully clarified vaccine misconceptions, alleviated the public's concerns, and substantially improved COVID-19 vaccine uptake.

Of course, not all stories are intended for the movable middle. If a student is delivering a narrative about how schools can improve youth mental health to a room of supporters, they should focus less on creating awareness about their issue and more on driving individual and collective action. Additional information about ways to effectively tailor a message for an intended audience can be found in Chapter 10.

3. **Show, don't tell.** Social impact stories often rely on words like equity, justice, and diversity to push their message. And while such concepts are valuable and necessary, they have also been politicized, which means explicit use of these terms can sometimes hinder consensus-building efforts (Niemand, 2018). In such instances, showing instead of telling can be highly effective.

When it comes to employing this strategy, novelist and screenwriter Richard Price said it best: "You don't write about the horrors of war. No. You write about a kid's burnt socks lying in the road." In the same way, a student who is eager to convey injustice when sharing a story about inequitable and inadequate school funding will be far more impactful and memorable if she uses visual language and personal stories to *show* rather than *tell* how school funding is inequitably and inadequately distributed. She'll write about the science textbooks from ten years ago with missing and ripped pages. She'll mention the teacher who works the weekend shift at a local coffee shop to make ends meet.

She'll highlight the students who have had three different math teachers in the same semester, the school counselor who doesn't have time to eat lunch, the cracked chairs and wobbly desks, the kid who can't take AP literature because it isn't offered at their school. She'll paint a picture of the student who always leaves his homework assignments buried at the bottom of his backpack, stuck together by last week's peanut butter sandwich, because no one is collecting them anyway.

In addition to the written word, visual mediums like art, photography, and video can be powerful tools through which to implement this strategy, allowing the audience to connect the dots and draw conclusions on their own.

The Public Narrative: Social Impact Storytelling in Action

Now that students have a foundational understanding of social impact storytelling, they are ready to put their knowledge and skills to practice by learning about and creating a public narrative. Developed by leadership scholar and community organizer Marshall Ganz (2011), a public narrative refers to the practice of transforming values into collective action in service of a shared purpose. A public narrative is not a script, but rather an iterative process that requires continuous telling, listening, and reflection.

> **Teaching Tip:**
>
> Consider sharing an example(s) of a public narrative with students or crafting your own. While countless public narrative examples can be found online, the most famous is undoubtedly Barack Obama's 2004 keynote address at the Democratic National Convention whereby he connected his personal story to the broader American story and highlighted shared challenges that required collective action.

The public narrative consists of three parts sequenced in no particular order: a story of self, a story of us, and a story of now. Taken together, public narratives connect one person's story (a story of self) to a broader story encompassing the shared aims and values of a community or organization (a story of us), translating them into a call for collective action (a story of now). In this section, we'll unpack each component of the public narrative and provide guiding questions for helping students begin to build their own.

- ♦ **A story of self** describes one's motivation for caring about or becoming involved in a given cause. A story of self often follows a basic narrative structure, consisting of a challenge the storyteller faced, the choice they made about how to navigate that challenge, and the outcome they experienced. Additional information about building a story of self can be found in Chapter 8: "The Story of Me."
- ♦ **A story of us** is a collective narrative that communicates a shared purpose, vision, and goals. The story of us invites others to join the effort.
- ♦ **A story of now** conveys a sense of urgency by describing current challenges, choices that must be made, and an aspirational vision for the future.

Guiding Questions for Building a Public Narrative

Story of Self

- ♦ What's your call to leadership?
- ♦ What experiences have compelled you to care about this issue(s)?
- ♦ If applicable, what is a challenge and a choice that led you to want to drive action around this issue(s)? What was the outcome of that choice?
- ♦ What makes you think you can make a difference?

Story of Us

- Who is your audience? Who is the "us" in the story of us?
- What shared experiences or values do you share with your audience?
- How can you identify and communicate a sense of shared values and purpose in your story?

Story of Now

- What change would you like to see in your school, your community, your state, your country, and/or the world?
- Why should your audience care? What shared challenges do they face and how might they benefit from responding to those challenges?
- How can listeners engage in action?

The process of creating a public narrative is a practice in both leadership and self-reflection, ultimately helping students—and educators—become more intentional about *how* and *why* they tell their stories.

Concluding Thoughts

So far, we've introduced the basics of social impact storytelling—from its historical origins to its contemporary applications—and reviewed concepts and strategies for effective story building and delivery. Now that students have a solid foundation upon which to build their storytelling skills, it's important to establish a trusting and respectful environment that opens the door to connection, community, and mutual understanding. That's precisely what we'll be covering in the next chapter—let's go!

Questions for Extended Student Dialogue

- How and to what extent, if at all, has your perspective of storytelling changed after learning about its connection to social change?
- In what ways do you intend to build consensus around your issue? What key points will you focus on?
- How might you incorporate ethos, pathos, and logos into your story?

Questions to Encourage Educator Self-Reflection

- What have you learned about storytelling as a result of this chapter? How has your perspective changed, if at all?
- Which concepts are students responding to with interest and enthusiasm? Which concepts, if any, are they grappling with?
- What social issues are students interested in focusing on?
- What additional support or resources do students need? What additional support and resources do you need?

References

Aje, L. (2013). Fugitive slave narratives and the (re)presentation of the self? The cases of Frederick Douglass and William Brown. *L'Ordinaire des Amériques*, 215. https://doi.org/10.4000/orda.507

Aristotle. (2005). *Poetics and rhetoric*. Barnes and Noble Classics.

Barraza, J. A., & Zak, P. J. (2009). Empathy toward strangers triggers oxytocin release and subsequent generosity. *Annals of the New York Academy of Sciences*, *1167*, 182–189.

Cartagena, J. (2004). When Bomba became the national music of the Puerto Rico Nation. *Centro Journal*, *16*(1), 14–35.

De Vos, G., Harris, M., & Lottridge, C. B. (2003). *Telling tales: Storytelling in the family*. University of Alberta Press.

Eagle, L., Dahl, S., & De Pelsmacker, P. (2020). *The Sage handbook of marketing ethics*. Sage Publications.

Ganz, M. (2011). Public narrative, collective action, and power. In S. Odugbemi & T. Lee (Eds.), *Accountability through public opinion: From inertia to public action* (pp. 273–289). The World Bank.

Gonzalez, M., Kokozos, M., Byrd C., & McKee, K. (2024). Storytelling through a critical positive youth development framework: A mixed methods approach. *Journal of Youth Development, 19*(1), 2.

Greenlee, C. (2024). The remarkable untold story of Sojourner Truth. *Smithsonian Magazine*. www.smithsonianmag.com/history/remarkable-untold-story-sojourner-truth-180983691/

Hechtkopf, K. (2010, February 11). Support for gays and lesbians in the military depends on the question. *CBS News*. www.cbsnews.com/news/support-for-gays-in-the-military-depends-on-the-question/

Katz, J. (1995). *The invention of heterosexuality*. Dutton.

Kendall-Taylor, N., & Gibbons, S. (2018, April 17). Framing for social change. *Stanford Social Innovation Review*. https://ssir.org/articles/entry/framing_for_social_change

King, Jr., M. L. (1968). *Remaining awake through a great revolution* [Speech transcript]. Howard Gotlieb Archival Research Center. https://kinginstitute.stanford.edu/king-papers/documents/remaining-awake-through-great-revolution-address-morehouse-college

Kirshner, B. (2015). *Youth activism in an era of education inequality*. New York University Press.

Kühberger, A. (1998). The influence of framing on risky decisions: A meta-analysis. *Organizational Behavior Human Decision Processes, 75*, 23–55. doi:10.1006/obhd.1998.2781

Lin, P. Y., Grewal, N. S., Morin, C., Johnson, W. D., & Zak, P. J. (2013). Oxytocin increases the influence of public service announcements. *PLoS ONE, 2*(2). doi:10.1371/journal.pone.0056934

Murchison, G. R., Agénor, M., Reisner, S. L., & Watson, R. J. (2019). School restroom and locker room restrictions and sexual assault risk among transgender youth. *Pediatrics, 143*(6). doi:10.1542/peds.2018-2902

Niemand, A. (2018, May 7). How to tell stories about complex issues. *Stanford Social Innovation Review*. https://ssir.org/articles/entry/how_to_tell_stories_about_complex_issues

Niemand, A. (2023, September 21). How to tell real stories about impact. *Stanford Social Innovation Review*. https://ssir.org/articles/entry/how_to_tell_real_stories_about_impact

Porter, J. (2013, October 25). Affordable care act or Obamacare: A lesson in framing. *Jeremy Porter Communications*. www.jrmyprtr.com/affordable-care-act-or-obamacare/

Romano, J. (1979, September 23). James Baldwin writing and talking. *New York Times*. www.nytimes.com/1979/09/23/archives/james-baldwin-writing-and-talking-baldwin-baldwin-authors-query.html

Sauer, M., & Limaye, R. (2021, March 18). *Building trust in vaccination*. John Hopkins Coronavirus Resource Center. https://coronavirus.jhu.edu/vaccines/report/building-trust-in-vaccination

Scholl, H. (1942). *Leaflets of the White Rose I*. The White Rose.

Search Institute. (2018). *Developmental assets among U.S. youth: 2018 update*. Search Institute.

Shulka, S. Y., Theobald, E. J., Abraham, J. K., & Price, R. M. (2022). Reframing educational outcomes: Moving beyond achievement gaps. *CBE—Life Sciences Education*, *21*(2). https://doi.org/10.1187/cbe.21-05-0130

Slovic, P. (2007). "If I look at the mass I will never act": Psychic numbing and genocide. *Judgment and Decision Making*, *2*(2), 79–95. https://doi.org/10.1017/S1930297500000061

Solomonian, L., & Di Ruggiero, E. (2021). The critical intersection of environmental and social justice: A commentary. *Global Health*, *17*(30). https://doi.org/10.1186/s12992-021-00686-4

Spitzer, T. B. (2020, February 22). *Sophie school and the White Rose*. The National WWII Museum. www.nationalww2museum.org/war/articles/sophie-scholl-and-white-rose

Starovoitov, S. (2021). *Narrating landscapes: How indigenous storytelling can unlock our environment's past*. State of the Planet. https://news.climate.columbia.edu/2021/09/02/narrating-landscapes-how-indigenous-storytelling-can-unlock-our-environments-past/

Umbreit, M. S., Vos, B., Coates, R. B., & Brown, K. (2003). *Facing violence: The path of restorative justice dialogue*. Criminal Justice Press.

World Health Organization. (2021, December 13). *Childhood cancer*. www.who.int/news-room/fact-sheets/detail/cancer-in-children

Yong, E. (2017, December 17). *The desirability of storytellers*. The Atlantic.

Zak, P. (2015). Why inspiring stories make us react: The neuroscience of narrative. *Cerebrum*, *2*, 1–13.

2

Trust, Community, and Connection

Laying the Groundwork for Authentic Storytelling

Let's revisit Nina, who we met in the previous chapter. A few months before sharing her story, Nina stepped into the classroom that would change her life. She was nervous, unsure about who her classmates would be and how they would treat her. Her teacher was nervous, too. Ms. Garcia wanted to integrate social impact storytelling into this year's English class. She'd read about how storytelling could nurture connection, increase student engagement and self-reflection, and empower students to use their voices to address the social issues they most cared about. But she also knew there was potential risk in asking students to share personal aspects about their lives, examine their biases, and engage in dialogue about complex social issues. Would she be able to build up enough trust that students would bring their authentic selves into the classroom and share their experiences in positive ways?

As educators, we must establish an environment where students can feel a sense of belonging. We can begin preparing

this space even before students arrive. In this chapter, we will explore the concept of belonging and describe how trust, community, and connection create a sense of belonging. Belonging is particularly critical in teaching social impact storytelling, where the narratives we explore are often deeply intertwined with personal identities, beliefs, and values. Students will be better prepared to navigate the process of storytelling if we as educators have a strong sense of who we are and what we believe and value. Otherwise, we may get stuck in our own biases and misinterpret students' stories, minimize their experiences, or otherwise create an environment that feels unsafe for authentic expression.

In storytelling spaces, students are not just sharing abstract ideas; they are often revealing vulnerable aspects of themselves. For example, when Nina spoke to her school, she wasn't merely delivering a lecture about addressing the needs of other students with disabilities. Instead, she was sharing her own lived experiences, some of which carried emotional weight and personal challenges. Through her story, she conveyed both her resilience and her deep desire for a school community that would fully embrace and include her. As educators guiding students through the process of telling such deeply personal stories, it is essential that we remain reflective and intentional in our approach, ensuring that the learning environment supports both the storyteller and the audience in meaningful and compassionate ways.

First, we'll lay the groundwork for effectively and intentionally teaching social impact storytelling. We'll then review the importance of building a community built on trust and connection and provide strategies for building a sense of belonging among students. Finally, we'll show how low-stakes storytelling activities can prepare students for critical reflection while strengthening their sense of belonging.

Preparing to Teach Storytelling

Teaching storytelling requires more than simply guiding students through narrative techniques; it demands that educators first

reflect on their own identities, experiences, and biases and foster students' ability to actively listen and express empathy for each other. The following recommendations are for you to keep in mind as you work with your students.

Modify activities based on students' needs, abilities, and learning styles. To maximize students' learning, consider asking them to write you a letter or complete an informal Google form with prompts such as: How do you learn best? What would make this class or program a positive experience for you? What, if anything, should I know about you as I am planning lessons and activities? What is one of your strengths? What do you like to do for fun? Then, use your knowledge of your students and your content area to make adaptations that will best serve your classroom. For example, if one of your students has mobility needs, think about how you might adapt activities to limit movement.

Such adaptations are core to the philosophy of Universal Design for Learning (UDL), a framework aimed at creating flexible learning environments that cater to the diverse needs of all learners. Research has consistently shown UDL's effectiveness in promoting inclusion and improving student outcomes (Almeqdad et al., 2023; Zhang et al., 2024). The UDL guidelines emphasize providing multiple means of representation, action, and expression to support learners with diverse abilities (CAST, 2018). For example, each student possesses unique learning preferences, and recognizing these can significantly impact their level of engagement and ability to demonstrate their learning. For example, some students may prefer visual storytelling—such as Instagram photos and YouTube videos—while others might enjoy written content like blog posts.

Autonomy and choice is highly encouraged as well. Research suggests that providing choices can enhance student motivation, self-efficacy, and overall academic performance (Mammadov & Schroeder, 2023; Mouratidis et al., 2024). Instead of adhering to traditional assessments like an essay or written story, consider offering a diverse menu of options. Students might choose to create a visual representation of their learning by giving a presentation, or even composing a song or poem. By honoring their individual preferences and strengths, you empower students to

express their understanding and storytelling abilities in ways that best suit their unique learning styles. We'll explore a variety of storytelling formats in Chapter 4.

Solicit feedback from students and incorporate their feedback into your planning. Feedback is the best way to understand how your adaptations are working for students and best meet their needs. Encouraging students to share their views and ideas also gives them a stake in their own learning. Feedback can take the form of anonymous exit tickets, a mid-term survey, or a quick check-in during class. The Stop-Start-Continue framework is a simple way to solicit focused feedback.

 Activity Spotlight: Stop-Start-Continue

Ask students:

1. What they would like to *stop* doing, or what isn't working well for them?
2. What would they like to do, maybe that they did in another class, that isn't currently happening?
3. What would they like to continue doing because they're enjoying it and/or it works well?

Ensure privacy and confidentiality, particularly when it comes to personal stories. Storytelling involves vulnerability and trust will be weakened if students find that something they shared in class is being told to others. Imagine a student telling a personal story that another student posts to social media where, instead of appreciation, they receive ridicule. Why would they open up in class ever again?

Make a plan to discuss community agreements that include guidelines around privacy and confidentiality, whether it's the Vegas Rule ("what happens here stays here") or a less stringent agreement like "take the learning, leave the stories." If you are a public school teacher, you are likely required by law to report when a student is experiencing an unsafe situation at home. Work

with your administrators and school counselors to understand the regulations and laws about what kinds of information must be shared outside of the classroom. Finally, make sure students are aware of your reporting responsibilities.

 Teaching Tip:

Community agreements create expectations or pathways for communication that prioritize care, respect, and trust within a group. Engage students in thinking about the kind of space *they* want and need to authentically and respectfully engage in dialogue and storytelling about complex social justice issues. First, ask students to think about and jot down their responses to the following prompts:

- How can we create an environment of mutual respect, care, and trust?
- What do we need to fully support and feel supported by each other in this group?
- What steps can we take to prioritize each other's well-being?
- How can we work through challenges or disagreements?

Once students have had enough time to think through these questions, divide them up into small groups and instruct them to draft a list of community agreements for dialogue and storytelling. Then, encourage groups to share their lists. Drawing on the responses, work with students to establish a collective set of community agreements, acknowledging that items can be adapted and additional agreements can be added as needed.

Pay attention to group dynamics. We have to work continuously to establish and preserve a sense of belonging and trust within the class. This means developing shared agreements about

discussions and enforcing those guidelines. It also means paying attention to who is and who is not speaking. Some students are naturally gregarious and ready to respond, while others will need time to process before they share their opinion. You'll want to make sure that you use activity formats that allow varied forms of engagement and provide opportunities for students to express themselves in their own ways. Similarly, students will come into the classroom with different friendships and can form cliques within the class. Intentional grouping practices can allow students to broaden their connections at times and deepen them at other times. For example, in our last summer camp, we noticed that four students had gotten very close on the first two days of camp, while another set of students tended to isolate themselves. Whenever we asked the campers to group up, the members of the clique always chose each other. On the third day, we had the campers count off so that each member of the clique went into a different group. That worked to expand the campers' attachments.

When putting students into groups, keep in mind relationships the students have outside your classroom and the potential for harm from pairing students with a bully or someone else they might feel uncomfortable with. Later in this chapter, we'll discuss how to respond to behavior that's not aligned with your community agreements.

An additional aspect of paying attention to group dynamics is paying attention to power. One source of power is our authority as the educators in the room. Storytelling and conversations about social issues can be exciting, and as a discussion leader, we can easily get caught up in the conversation. We might have strong opinions about some topics or the conversation might lead us to important insights of our own. We have to be careful that we are not centering our ideas in the discussions and that our contributions are not pushing students' thinking to the side. It may be tempting to make a particular point, but the point will be more powerful if students come to the realization on their own.

For example, Tori was leading an after-school program for teen girls and was becoming frustrated with a discussion the girls were having about make-up.

"I think it's fine if anyone chooses to wear make-up, I don't have a problem with it," Sophia said.

"Yeah," Harper said, "people should be able to do whatever they want."

Tori knew both girls wore make-up every day and had seen them teasing other girls about not wearing it. She, herself, was teased as a teen and knew how painful it could be. "Well, what do other people think?" Tori asked, hoping some of the quieter girls would speak up. No one did. "Well, don't you think it's not so easy to be different from others?" she said.

"I think everybody feels like they can wear it if they want," Sophia insisted.

"Well, not everyone feels that way. You should really think about how other girls feel. When I was a kid..." The more Tori talked, the more Sophia and Harper disengaged, while the quieter girls looked at her in dismay. After a few minutes, Tori stopped and took a breath, noticing that her heart was pounding. "Who else has an opinion?" she asked. The group was silent in response.

Being clear about the learning goals and the evidence for the goals can be helpful as you are facilitating discussions. If Tori's goal was to have an open conversation, she should try to be OK with the outcome even if she disagrees. If, on the other hand, she wanted the girls to appreciate the pressures other girls might face, she could have structured the conversation, for example by having girls list reasons people do and do not choose to wear make-up. Then she could have made sure peer pressure was mentioned.

Tori also let her personal feelings shape how she wanted the conversation to go instead of trusting the students to lead and come to their own conclusions. While her feelings are relevant and valuable, it's more useful to process them with a group of adult peers and be prepared to share the results of her learning in an *intentional* and appropriate way.

As the program leader, Tori had more power than the students, so they were likely hesitant to interrupt or contradict her. Similarly, students with privileged identities—those who hold societal advantages due to factors such as race, gender,

socioeconomic status, or ability—often feel more comfortable speaking up because they are accustomed to environments where their perspectives are validated and supported. A white, male student from a middle-class background may be more vocal in class discussions, feeling confident that his viewpoints align with the dominant culture. Meanwhile, a student of color or a student from a low-income background might hesitate to share, fearing that their experiences will not be understood or valued. We must be aware of these dynamics and ensure that they do not stifle students' voices. Instead, we want to create an environment where all students feel encouraged to contribute in a meaningful way.

Continuously take stock of how your values, positionality, lived experiences, and biases shape your pedagogical lens. For those of us who grew up in middle class communities, the kinds of stories our middle class students tell will be more familiar to us. We might even feel uncomfortable hearing about the experiences of lower income students. At these times we need to ask ourselves: Why am I uncomfortable? What kinds of assumptions am I making?

We'll also need to be mindful of how our comfort or tendencies can lead us to elevate certain perspectives and leave others' out. When giving examples, we might find it easier to talk about experiences from our own childhood, which could exclude students who don't share our background. You might enjoy hearing about students' summer vacations and sharing your favorite amusement park rides. However, some of your students may have spent their summer helping their family with work or caring for younger siblings instead of traveling. Without extra effort on your part, those students might feel like you aren't as interested in them or that they aren't as welcome. By intentionally bringing multiple perspectives into our community, we can challenge ourselves and honor students' varied backgrounds.

Keep in mind, however, that it is not the responsibility of students to educate their peers. Some teachers will single out

the one Jewish student in the classroom to talk about Hanukkah during winter. Putting students on the spot can make them feel like they have to speak on behalf of an entire group or feel like their entire experience has been reduced to one identity. Instead, we can find content on Hanukkah to present and give the opportunity for all students to share about their winter holiday plans. A Jewish student may want to add something, or they may quietly appreciate having their background represented.

All of these recommendations relate to your developing critical reflection. As we noted in our guiding principles, *critical reflection is a prerequisite for students and educators* engaged in the process of social impact storytelling. Critical reflection is our awareness of the social, political, and economic forces that shape our lives and communities. This means understanding that marginalized groups face prejudice and discrimination both at the individual level and at institutional and structural levels. Historical and social forces have worked so that privileged groups have benefited from these unequal structures.

Keep in mind that the ways that these forces manifest will be unique to our local context and will change over time. This means critical reflection is a process, not a destination. However, in order to be effective at guiding our students through their critical reflection journey, we'll need to be a few steps ahead of them and willing to do our work outside of our classrooms or community organizations. We don't want our lack of knowledge to come at the expense of a student's feelings or ask students to educate us. Otherwise, we may hinder students' growth and undermine the very trust and connection we aim to foster.

Critical reflection requires regular self-reflection. In this book, the end of each chapter includes "Questions to Encourage Facilitator Self-Reflection." Make sure you spend time on these questions. Don't just think about them, keep a handwritten or digital journal where you can fully explore each one. Consider writing a reflection at the end of each class meeting where you think about what went well, what challenged you, and what you will do in the next meeting.

> **Tips for Educators: Developing Your Critical Reflection**
>
> - Take a workshop or read about social justice issues. The reference section of this chapter lists some of our favorite books.
> - Read autobiographies and essays by people from diverse backgrounds.
> - Visit history museums and cultural centers to learn about the cultural groups in your area.
> - Read books on the history and culture of groups you're unfamiliar with.
> - Explore your own cultural background by talking with your family and elders in your community.
> - Participate respectfully in social media spaces or a community organization dedicated to social issues facing a particular group. If you are a person who doesn't belong to that group, pay careful attention to the group norms and know when to speak up and when to listen.
> - Make friends with people from different backgrounds. Don't ask them to teach you their language or their culture, but be open to what they share with you.
> - Notice whenever you're uncomfortable and think about why.

Once we've prepared ourselves to lead students in social impact storytelling, it's time to set up our community as a place where everyone feels trust, community, and connection.

Building Belonging

Telling authentic and ethical stories means being true to who we are and where we come from. In order to get to a place where we can tell those authentic stories, we have to trust the people around us. We have to believe that our peers will listen actively and respectfully, that they will respond to our stories

with affirmation and support rather than skepticism and ridicule. We want those around us to value us because of what we have shared with them and in return to share parts of themselves with us. This requires a connected community where we feel respected, appreciated, and supported, where we have a sense of belonging.

When we're trying to figure out whether we belong to a community, we make observations and ask questions like "Does anyone here even notice me?" "Are there people here with whom I connect?" "Do people here value (people like) me?" "Is this a setting in which I want to belong?" "Can I be more than a stereotype here?" and "Are people like me incompatible with this setting or behavior?" (Walton & Brady, 2017). When students' personal experiences are invited into the classroom and become the content of classroom discussion, the answers to those questions are clearly YES!

Building a sense of belonging is especially important for students with marginalized identities because these students are more likely to experience classroom environments as places where they do not fit in and where people like them are not welcome. Educators can address these students' concerns by making it clear that their lived experiences, their previous knowledge, and their communities are an important part of the learning environment (Gray et al., 2020).

Imagine a student named Alina, whose family immigrated to the US and who often felt like her background set her apart from her peers. One day in her social studies class, the teacher encouraged students to share stories related to their family's migration experiences. Alina hesitated at first, unsure of whether her story was worth sharing. Her family wasn't from Mexico, India, or China. Some of her classmates didn't even know she hadn't been born in the US. Still, after hearing her classmates share their stories, she decided to talk about her family's journey. To her surprise, everyone listened to her. Her classmates made connections to their own experiences and asked thoughtful questions about the differences in their experiences. Her teacher was able to relate Alina's story to the broader themes for the day's topic. At the end of that period, Alina felt seen, valued, and

connected. She realized that her story added something unique to the classroom and that she belonged there, not in spite of her background but because of it.

It's not always easy to build belonging, however. In Ms. Garcia's first year of teaching, she assigned a family tree activity to help students think about their heritage and make the point that all humans are a family. One student refused to do the activity because his parents were divorced. Another student, who had been adopted, got upset because the tree template only had space for two parents, not four. That student's adoptive mother complained to the principal, who told Ms. Garcia not to do any more "family" activities. Even though Ms. Garcia wanted to bring her students' backgrounds into the classroom, she never did anything like that activity again.

So how can you build a sense of belonging while remaining sensitive to students' unique circumstances? In the next section, we will describe some suggestions and activities to build connection and community by helping students get to know each other in positive, affirming ways.

Creating Community

Our CPYD model and guiding principles introduced some key considerations for teaching storytelling in classrooms and communities. Here, we return to the idea that *space matters*. Belonging scholar Keonya Booker (2021) interviewed nine high school teachers to explore how they built trust, community, and connection—all vital to belonging—in their classrooms. She distilled her findings into four overarching themes: caring, consistency, contracts, and challenges.

Caring: Just as in the CPYD model, caring educators show empathy, compassion, and an interest in students' lives in and outside of the classroom. Teachers in Booker's (2021) study recognized that their tone of voice and whether they corrected students publicly or in private was useful in showing empathy and building positive relationships with students. For teens especially, attention from peers can override academic concerns, so a private correction can help them save face and still improve their behavior.

Consistency: Trust is stronger when educators are honest and reliable. Consistent educators back up their words with action and establish a predictable environment with regular routines. Structure is especially important for youth who have been previously disappointed by a lack of support at home. When students know what to expect, the community can also recover from unexpected events more quickly. For example, a teacher in the study always kept a stock of sharpened pencils at his desk. When a student was missing a pencil, he would give the student one and avoid delays from digging for supplies or going to the pencil sharpener. Although it placed a burden on the teacher, it saved valuable time and showed the students he was someone they could rely on.

Contracts: Another aspect of consistency is clearly conveying expectations for behavior and enforcing consequences for not meeting expectations. Some use the term "boundaries" instead of "rules" (Booker, 2021) to highlight the idea that students have autonomy and choice regarding their behavior. In this book, we refer to these expectations as community agreements. When we ask students to co-create community agreements, they feel a greater sense of accountability for their actions (Bowen et al., 2022). One teacher in Booker's (2021) study discussed questions such as "What do you expect of your teacher and of yourself? What are things that should not ever happen here?" (p. 75). Once set, the agreements need to be consistently enforced and modified when necessary. And remember that it's just as important that we as adults model the agreements and engage respectfully with students instead of being aggressive or defensive. We must take feedback and be willing to apologize if we make a mistake.

 Teaching Tip:

1. **Set clear guidelines early:** Establish community agreements around respect, confidentiality, and active listening. Encourage students to approach sensitive topics with empathy and open-mindedness.

2. **Model vulnerability and accountability:** Share your own experiences with challenging topics to normalize discomfort in learning and growth. At the same time, be open to feedback and admit when you might have misstepped, modeling how to handle sensitive discussions with humility.
3. **Create space for reflection:** Allow time for personal reflection before and after discussing heavy or divisive topics. This could be through journaling, a quiet moment, or small group discussions. This helps students process their emotions and thoughts in a less confrontational space.
4. **Acknowledge discomfort:** Don't shy away from acknowledging that certain topics may be triggering. Encourage students to share their concerns with you privately if they feel overwhelmed. If a topic becomes too overwhelming for a student, provide options for them to engage with the material in a way that feels safer without compromising the learning goals of the course.
5. **Debrief after discussions:** Ask students how they are feeling, what they learned, and what they still need. This reinforces that these topics require ongoing engagement and care.

By showing caring, being consistent, and enforcing your contracts, difficult conversations can be productive learning opportunities.

Challenges: Youth face a number of challenges in classrooms and educational spaces, including social media and cell phone use. About 95% of teens have smartphones, and more than half report using TikTok, Snapchat, and Instagram on a daily basis (Pew Research Center, 2023). We have to think carefully about how to manage the fallout when conflicts on social media spill into the classroom. A strategy one teacher used was to assign students to peer feedback sessions as a way to encourage

positive interactions while supporting formative assessment (Booker, 2021).

Another challenge can be students' behavior. For example, during an activity where they are talking about their cultural background, a Black student named Denise said, "Something people say to me is that I talk white. I don't even know what that means. This is just how I talk."

Kevin, another Black student, piped up, "You do talk kind of white, though." Others in the class laughed.

What should we do in these kinds of situations? Should we say something? What if you're not Black? Will we offend the students if we intervene?

Whenever there is a violation of the class agreements, we must respond. As an authority figure in the room, students are looking to us to know whether the agreements are important or if they were an empty exercise. First, you will want to acknowledge the harm that has occurred or potentially occurred and reinforce the class agreements. In the case of Denise and Kevin, the educator could say, "Denise was really kind to share her experience with us. In our class guidelines, we said we wanted to be respectful, and Kevin, your comment did not sound respectful to me."

It's possible that Denise may laugh along with her peers or say, "It's not a big deal," even if it is. She may not want to draw further attention or feel like a bad sport. The important thing is that you, the leader of the community, drew attention to the potential disruption.

Next, we restore the community as appropriate. Follow through on whatever consequences you have in your classroom and quickly return to the topic at hand. Depending on the violation and the consequences in your classroom, you may ask the student to withdraw in some way. For some students, a verbal reminder is enough. Keep in mind that if the punishment for violating a classroom agreement is too severe, you may stifle discussion because students are too afraid of saying the wrong thing.

Note that we don't need to know what Denise meant about "talking white" and we don't need to ask a Black colleague about language norms in the Black community. If it's something the educator wants to address later, she could. Kevin's comment

could be an interesting opening to talk about identity and language. However, the first priority should be the well-being and safety of students and the preservation of the community.

Finally, students may also be struggling with mental health and identity concerns and may not have supportive adults at home. By building a caring and connected learning environment, we can meet some of students' basic needs and free their attention for learning. Of course you will not be able to meet all of the students' needs, but you can cultivate a space that actively prioritizes equity, belonging, and wellness. As Nissa, a Spanish teacher, put it, "There are a whole lot of things outside of school that we can't control, but we can control what happens when they walk into our room" (Booker, 2021, p. 78).

Storytelling for Connection

We believe that personal storytelling is an important tool in building a connected community. In a later chapter, we'll go into detail about the foundations of personal storytelling and how it can nurture critical reflection and empower students to be change agents. Here, we explain how low-stakes storytelling opportunities can build trust, community, and connection by helping students get to think about who they are and where they come from, and to share those parts of themselves with others. Through these activities, students get to know their classmates and begin to develop their critical reflection by noticing patterns between and across identities. You may have done some of these activities before. We'll discuss why they are effective for creating a sense of belonging among students. Note that each of these activities requires a level of vulnerability, so later in the chapter we'll discuss more about how cultivating a culture of trust creates space for openness and learning.

 Activity Spotlight: Concentric Circles

In this activity, students stand in two circles, one inside the other, with each person in the inner circle facing one person in the outer circle. Read a prompt and ask each pair to discuss the prompt for two to three minutes. When time is up,

ask one circle to rotate so that each person has a new partner. Give the next prompt and time to discuss, then rotate again. Continue for several rounds. Some example prompts are:

- What is your favorite meal?
- What's something you are proud of?
- Talk about a person (or animal) that makes you smile
- What place are you looking forward to going soon?

Make sure the prompts are personal and give each person the chance to share something meaningful.

Students share who they are as individuals. In an activity like concentric circles, students get the chance to talk about a topic they know well: themselves! Since everyone shares, everyone can feel like they are noticed and valued (Walton & Brady, 2017). This brief conversation can spark a friendship based on shared interests. Students realize there are people they can connect to (Walton & Brady, 2017). At the same time, the few minutes with each partner reduces the worry about not having enough to say or feeling uncertain about talking to someone new.

 Activity Spotlight: I Am From Poem

This activity is inspired by George Ella Lyon's poem, "I Am From." Start by reading Lyon's poem or other "I Am From" poems from https://iamfromproject.com and consider sharing the student example below. Next, ask students to write a list of memories, people, places, and things that are important to them, such as:

- Foods they eat with their families
- Sights, sounds, and smells from their home and community
- Sayings, words, and phrases common to their family

Then ask students to use their lists to write their own poems, starting each line with "I am from…" Templates are also available online. Invite students to read their poems aloud.

I Am From

Anonymous

> I am from old downtowns,
> gentrified mills,
> churches on every corner,
> The happeningest place in the county.
> I am from collard greens,
> sweet potato pie,
> macaroni and cheese,
> Every Sunday is a holiday meal.
> I am from Carowinds,
> Myrtle Beach,
> camping in the mountains,
> A new adventure in each season.
> I am from books,
> just 10 per week,
> spaceships and magicians,
> Entire worlds explored deep into the night.

Students share what they value about their backgrounds. Activities that recognize who students are as individuals can be complemented by activities that allow students to share about their families and cultural background. These activities help students share their unique perspectives while showing them similarities across experiences. Sometimes we assume that we can't find much in common with someone who is from a very different background, but one of us authors was surprised and pleased to bond with a student from another country over what he called *chichas* and she called *chittlins* (cooked pig intestines). By sharing our backgrounds, we can challenge assumptions and stereotypes about other cultures and help students appreciate our common humanity. This answers the question of whether people like them are valued (Walton &

Brady, 2017). These activities will not teach students much about a culture's history, traditions, or values, but they will pave the way for curiosity and deeper learning. More importantly, they help students build trust and connections with each other.

> **Teaching Tip:**
>
> To avoid challenges like Ms. Garcia's experience with the family tree activity, choose activities that do not make assumptions about students' backgrounds or family structures. Not all students come from two-parent households, live with biological relatives, or take summer vacations. Be mindful that culture is complex, and students may identify with their race, ethnicity, and cultures in diverse and personal ways.
>
> One activity we recommend is the **I Am Poem**, referenced earlier in this chapter, which allows students to reflect on meaningful memories from their everyday lives (such as foods, smells, or sayings). This approach enables students to express what matters most to them without feeling stereotyped or boxed in.
>
> Remember, students often infer whether they belong in a space by asking themselves, "Can I be more than a stereotype here?" (Walton & Brady, 2017). By centering activities on what students value about their backgrounds, you create space for genuine expression and honor their unique identities.

Students learn to actively listen. The personal storytelling we'll discuss later demands "listening to witness" (Bernal et al., 2006; Freire, 1970; Machado, 2023). Early storytelling is also a time to help students practice this skill. *Listening to witness* means that we go beyond merely hearing—we are making a conscious effort to bear witness to the storyteller's narrative, emotions, and the sociohistorical context from which their experiences emerge (Guajardo et al., 2016; Khalifa, 2018). Listening to witness requires suspending judgment, redefining power dynamics, and

embracing vulnerability (Gutiérrez, 2016). We ask our students to adopt this stance by engaging with their peers through a lens of empathy, sensitivity, criticality, and openness. Teaching this skill helps students know this community is a place where their peers are expected to notice and appreciate them, helping to answer the question "Is this a setting in which I want to belong?" (Walton & Brady, 2017).

 Activity Spotlight: Listening to Witness

First define "listening to witness" and ask students to list examples of what this active, intentional listening style looks like. Next, place students into pairs. Have them choose one person to be the speaker and one the listener. The speaker will respond to a prompt for two minutes without interruption while their partner "listens to witness." Choose prompts that are meaningful to your class content or ask students to tell a story about themselves. When the two minutes are up, the listener can ask questions, reflect back feelings, and paraphrase for an additional minute. Then the pair will switch roles. The new speaker will speak for two minutes and then their partner will reflect back for one minute.

Debrief the activity with questions such as:

- As the speaker, what did it feel like to know that the listener was fully engaged and present?
- As a listener, what did you pick up that you normally might have missed?
- As the listener, how well did you maintain nonverbal communication, paraphrase information, and ask questions to elicit additional information?
- Was it difficult to actively listen and not respond? Why or why not?
- How has this activity changed your perspective on listening?

It's the second week of Ms. Garcia's class and she's still a little nervous about the students. So far they seem to enjoy the activities but have been hesitant to share too personally. She has the students do the "listening to witness" activity and asks, "How did it go?"

"Awkward!"

"I had no idea what to talk about for two minutes."

"I hate talking about myself."

She calls on Jamal, who thinks for a moment. Then he says, "I liked it. I don't think anyone's ever really listened to me like that before." Ms. Garcia sees a new light in his eyes. She thinks this just might work.

Trust: Managing the Risks of Vulnerability

In the previous section we described how storytelling can help students develop a sense of belonging by talking about themselves, by sharing their backgrounds, and by "listening to witness" (Machado, 2023). However, the emotional depth of these activities often hinges on the storyteller's willingness to be vulnerable, which opens them up to potential harm. Sharing personal or family stories can feel risky (Machado, 2023). Students may worry that their story isn't compelling, that their emotions will be too raw, or that their peers won't be able to relate to their experience. Even where community agreements are in place, there is always the possibility that students may not listen respectfully or, as in Kevin's teasing response to Denise, that they may even react with hurtful comments.

We cannot make any community a completely safe space. However, we can prepare students to engage in ways that promote safety, model community agreements, and repair harm when it occurs. One important strategy is to validate students' efforts to open up. A simple "thank you for sharing" or "I appreciate hearing your story" can go a long way in reinforcing the value of vulnerability. As McAdams (1993) highlights, personal narratives that embody our emotions—whether they evoke joy, sorrow, or frustration—deepen our understanding of the human experience. Sharing these stories helps build a classroom community where students feel seen and valued (Gay, 2018; Gray et al.,

2020). Vulnerability, as Baldwin and Linnea (2010) note, allows storytellers to tap into the power of their stories by creating authentic connections that foster new understandings among peers. Machado (2023), for example, found that when students shared stories about personal traditions and experiences, it strengthened the bonds within the community.

Brown (2015) also argues that experiencing empathy through connection and empowerment can counteract feelings of isolation and powerlessness. When students are able to share their vulnerabilities with trustworthy, responsive classmates, it creates opportunities for connection that are free from secrecy, silence, or judgment. In being vulnerable, students can become more open with themselves and others, fostering a sense of belonging and trust.

That said, educators must also be mindful of the potential risks and challenges associated with asking students to be vulnerable. Be aware of potential triggers and set clear boundaries around how personal sharing will unfold in the classroom. Some students may not feel comfortable sharing certain aspects of their identity, particularly if they come from marginalized backgrounds, such as LGBTQIA+ students. Others may struggle with the concept of vulnerability because they don't recognize their own privilege and may take for granted the safety they feel in being seen as individuals. At the same time, it's important not to assume what a student does or doesn't want to share. Instead, honor their agency by offering opportunities to challenge themselves to be vulnerable, while simultaneously respecting their boundaries and the limits of what they feel safe disclosing. You might feel nervous when a student plans to talk about their incarcerated parent, but the student might feel proud to share their parent's commitment to turning their life around.

The storytelling methods discussed in this book won't erase the potential for harm or make vulnerability any less risky. However, they offer a powerful pathway for building trust, community, and connection. As educators engaged in social justice work, our goal is to help create a world where people can be their authentic selves with their full potential recognized and celebrated. This work requires the skill to see the humanity in others and to respond with empathy and compassion. These

skills don't develop overnight; they take practice, reflection, and the cultivation of a community where everyone is valued for their own memories, their own emotions, and their own truth. You can create that world in your classroom right now.

Concluding Thoughts

Before Kayleigh even begins sharing her story, she starts crying. Ms. Garcia gives the class a break and asks Kayleigh if she wants to continue. Kayleigh says yes, but Ms. Garcia is concerned. She'd read Kayleigh's story beforehand and thought it would be appropriate for her to share with the class. But if Kayleigh is so upset now, maybe there's something else she'll talk about? Will the rest of the class be upset? Before Ms. Garcia can do anything else, Kayleigh starts sharing. When she finishes her story, she's crying again. Some of the other classmates have glossy eyes, too. Maya reaches out and holds Kayleigh's hand. For a moment, the class sits in silence. Ms. Garcia is still worried, but when she takes the moment to feel the silence, she realizes it's an appreciative silence. The class is connected in a way they weren't a short while ago. At the end of the day, Kayleigh says, "Thanks for making us do that activity. I thought it was going to be cringe, but it was all right." Ms. Garcia encourages her to meet with the school counselor, just in case. Later that week, Ms. Garcia sees Kayleigh and Maya sitting, heads together, making plans to hang out after school.

Young people (and people in general) seek acceptance and may not always realize how eager we are, as educators, not only to accept but to celebrate who they are and support their growth into the best versions of themselves. In this chapter, we've outlined key principles to help you prepare for teaching social impact storytelling, emphasizing the importance of trust, community, and connection. We also discussed how storytelling activities can foster a sense of belonging before reflecting on the challenges of vulnerability. In the next chapter, we will describe more low-stakes activities for continuing to foster community while helping students grow more comfortable with the idea of storytelling.

Questions for Extended Student Dialogue

- Can you share a time when you felt you truly belonged to a community? What made that experience special for you?
- How do you feel when you share something personal in class? How does it affect your connection to your classmates?
- How can we support each other in this classroom to ensure everyone feels valued and heard?
- How do stereotypes and biases shape our interactions with others, and what can we do to challenge and overcome them?
- Why is it important to bring emotions, identities, families, and communities into our classroom discussions?
- In what ways can sharing our personal stories contribute to social change and a more just society?

Questions to Encourage Facilitator Self-Reflection

- What assumptions and biases might I bring into the classroom, and how can I work to recognize and address them?
- How do I respond to students' stories to ensure they feel heard and valued?
- How do my own experiences with privilege and marginalization influence my approach to facilitating discussions on social justice?
- What strategies can I use to ensure that all students' voices are heard and valued, especially those from marginalized backgrounds?

- How can I model vulnerability and openness in a way that encourages students to do the same?
- How can I continually improve my approach to facilitating discussions on social justice to better support my students' growth and understanding?

References

Almeqdad, Q. I., Alodat, A. M., Alquraan, M. F., Mohaidat, M. A., & Al-Makhzoomy, A. K. (2023). The effectiveness of Universal Design for Learning: A systematic review of the literature and meta-analysis. *Cogent Education, 10*(1), 2218191.

Baldwin, C., & Linnea, A. (2010). *The circle way: A leader in every chair*. Berrett-Koehler Publishers.

Bernal, D. D., Elenes, C. A., Godinez, F. E., & Villenas, S. (Eds.). (2006). *Chicana/Latina education in everyday life: Feminista perspectives on pedagogy and epistemology*. State University of New York Press.

Booker, K. (2021). Rules without relationships lead to rebellion: Secondary teachers and school belonging. *School Community Journal, 31*(1), 65–84.

Bowen, C. L., Hudson, H., Austin, S. J., Landaiche, C., Peters, A. M., Salom, M. F., & Morand, B. (2022, October). The development and implementation of class community norms to facilitate learning in a social justice-oriented classroom. In *2022 IEEE Frontiers in Education Conference (FIE)* (pp. 1–9). IEEE.

Brown, B. (2015). *Daring greatly: How the courage to be vulnerable transforms the way we live, love, parent, and lead*. Penguin.

CAST. (2018). *Universal Design for Learning guidelines version 2.2*. CAST.

Freire, P. (1970). *Pedagogy of the oppressed* (M. B. Ramos, Trans.). Continuum.

Gay, G. (2018). *Culturally responsive teaching: Theory, research, and practice*. Teachers College Press.

Gray, D. L., Hope, E. C., & Byrd, C. M. (2020). Why Black adolescents are vulnerable at school and how schools can provide opportunities to belong to fix it. *Policy Insights from the Behavioral and Brain Sciences, 7*(1), 3–9.

Guajardo, M., Guajardo, F., Janson, C., & Militello, M. (2016). *Reframing community partnerships in education: Uniting the power of place and wisdom of people*. Routledge.

Gutiérrez, K. D. (2016). Developing a sociocritical literacy in the third space. *Reading Research Quarterly, 43*(2), 148–164.

Khalifa, M. (2018). *Culturally responsive school leadership.* Harvard Education Press.

Machado, M. (2023). Family stories matter: Critical pedagogy of storytelling in elementary classrooms. *VUE (Voices in Urban Education), 51*(1). doi:10.35240/vue.26

Mammadov, S., & Schroeder, K. (2023). A meta-analytic review of the relationships between autonomy support and positive learning outcomes. *Contemporary Educational Psychology, 75*, 102235.

McAdams, D. P. (1993). *The stories we live by: Personal myths and the making of the self.* William Morrow.

Mouratidis, A., Michou, A., Koçak, A., Alp Christ, A., & Selçuk, Ş. (2024). The interplay between autonomy support and structure in the prediction of challenge-seeking, novelty avoidance, and procrastination. *Educational Psychology, 44*(8), 803–822.

Pew Research Center. (2023, December). *Teens, social media and technology 2023.* www.pewresearch.org/internet/2023/12/11/teens-social-media-and-technology-2023/

Walton, G. M., & Brady, S. T. (2017). The many questions of belonging. In A. J. Elliot, C. S. Dweck, & D. S. Yeager (Eds.), *Handbook of competence and motivation: Theory and application* (2nd ed., pp. 272–293). The Guilford Press.

Zhang, L., Carter, R. A. Jr., Greene, J. A., & Bernacki, M. L. (2024). Unraveling challenges with the implementation of Universal Design for Learning: A systematic literature review. *Educational Psychology Review, 36*(1), 35.

3

Ready, Set, Warm-Up

Activities for Awakening the Storyteller Within

By now, we've learned about the pedagogical, social, and emotional benefits of critically grounded storytelling. We've also reviewed the theoretical frameworks that shape social impact stories. In this chapter and the one that follows, we'll build on the *how* of storytelling and dig into additional pedagogical strategies and applications for effective and scaffolded facilitation.

Let's get started by demystifying who storytelling is for. Many people assume that storytelling is reserved for extroverts, performers, and the creatively inclined. This assumption can make the prospect of creating and delivering a story intimidating, especially for students. So how can we, as educators, ease students into the storytelling process in a way that builds self-confidence, nurtures connection, and gets their creative and introspective juices flowing? We find that warm-up activities can be helpful and we're sharing some of our favorites below.

> **Teaching Tip:**
>
> Active listening is an important and necessary part of the storytelling exchange. Wherever students are in their process, continue to practice active listening. Revisit Chapter 2 for additional information and activities related to active listening and "listening to witness."

My 30 Second Story

My 30 Second Story is exactly what it sounds like: an opportunity for students to pack as much about themselves as possible into a 30 second vignette, whether a montage of interesting facts, a retelling of their favorite memory, or a play-by-play of their morning routine. Once you've modeled the activity with your own 30 second story, give students ample time—five minutes is typically sufficient—to craft 30 seconds of content, which translates into about six to eight short sentences.

This activity, developed by co-author of this book, Michael Kokozos, works well as a community-building exercise but can also be used in a variety of other contexts. The structure and content of the 30 second story is up to each student so long as the focus is on themselves. The 30 second time limit is also flexible; it can be extended or shortened at your discretion. Using a timer is optional, but we recommend one. It can be part of the fun (and the challenge) of the 30 second story!

> **Teaching Tip:**
>
> Most 30 second stories students share will be vignettes rather than stories, as they won't follow a narrative arc

> with a clear beginning, middle, and end. Use this activity as an opportunity to distinguish between stories and vignettes.

Blackout Poetry

Blackout poetry is a fun and effective way to boost students' creativity and nurture their self-confidence as poets and storytellers. This method, popularized by writer Austin Kleon (2014), allows students to create poetry using a page of existing text from a newspaper, magazine, or book. What makes blackout poetry especially inviting is that students don't actually have to *write* anything; they simply have to choose the words or short phrases in the selected text that most resonate, circle them, and arrange the words into a poem. Remaining words are "blacked out" using a permanent marker.

To facilitate this activity, you'll need old books, magazines, and newspapers that students can rip apart and repurpose; alternatively, you can print digital pages from articles, online magazines, and classic books in the public domain. You'll also want to provide students with pencils and erasers. Don't forget colored pencils and markers, as some students may want to illustrate their blackout poems or add a pop of color.

Once students are done, encourage them to share their poems in pairs or as a large group. Ask students about their process for creating their poem: How did they choose which words to circle? What is the overall theme of their poem? What do they hope readers will take away from their poem? What, if anything, did they learn about themselves?

You can also facilitate a gallery walk activity by hanging students' poems around the classroom or community space and giving them time to read each other's work, ask questions, and provide feedback.

64 ◆ Teaching Storytelling in Classrooms and Communities

Below is a student-created blackout poem.

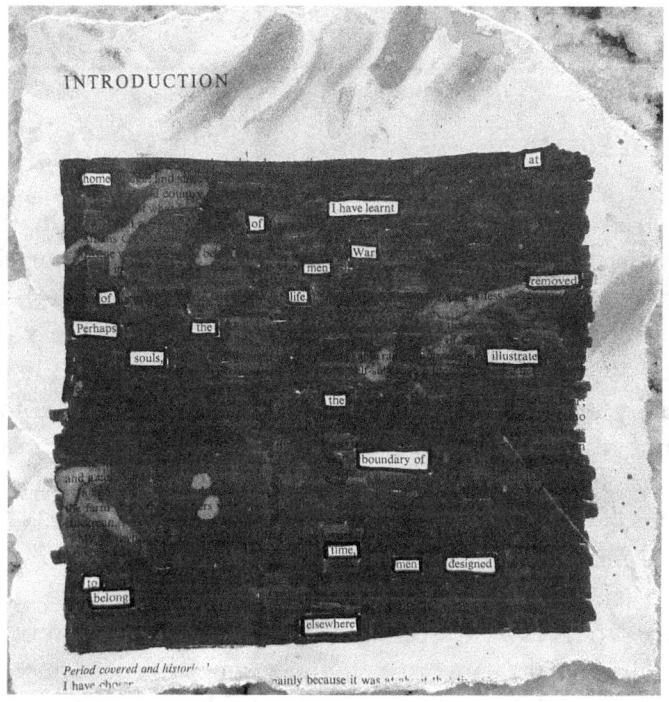

Created by Kearns Trotter

The text reads:

> at home
> I have learned
> of War
> men removed
> of life
> Perhaps the souls
> illustrate
> the boundary of
> time
> men designed
> to belong elsewhere

Storytelling Prompts

Storytelling prompts are questions and activities that generate dialogue and informally engage students in the storytelling exchange. Prompts help students become comfortable identifying and sharing their ideas without the pressure that often accompanies the prolonged preparation of storybuilding. Here are a few of our favorite storytelling prompts:

- Tell me about a time when...
  - Divide students into groups of two and ask them to share a short 30 second to two minute story detailing their recollection of a specific event. Prompts should be specific, like *Tell me about a time you felt proud of yourself.* Give students two to three minutes to think about their story followed by time to share their stories with one another using active listening skills.
- Group story
  - A group story starts with a sentence or idea. Students then take turns contributing to the story with a word, phrase, or short sentence. We might start with a simple sentence like *Sam was having a bad day at school.* We could then instruct students to add to this story with the narrative arc in mind. Specifically, what challenge(s) is Sam facing that is causing him to have a bad day? What choice does he make in response to that challenge? How might he find a resolution?
  - We may also opt for a prompt that's structured more like a group commentary. For example, students could each complete a sentence stem like, *My vision of a truly inclusive and equitable school is...* Students could then commit to an action step by responding to a second prompt, like this one: *I will contribute to such a vision by...*
- Additional questions that spark dialogue and reflection

- There is no shortage of relevant and thought-provoking questions we can use to spark creativity, self-reflection, and dialogue. Below are a couple of our favorite (and free!) resources to get you started:
  - *The Learning Network* provides teaching and learning resources based on content from the *New York Times*, including more than 1,000 writing prompts.
  - *StoryCorps*, a non-profit organization dedicated to sharing and preserving people's stories, has resources to facilitate storytelling within the classroom and in youth-serving organizations.

Crowdsourced Poetry

A crowdsourced poem is a collection of words and phrases submitted by multiple people in relation to a specific theme or issue. The innately collaborative nature of crowdsourced poetry lends itself to community building, which is an important function of storytelling in a classroom setting. Additionally, crowdsourced poetry is a low-stakes way to engage students in creative self-expression. Based on our experience, we find that students are much more likely to share two lines of a larger collaborative poem than a solo-authored piece. As with all sharing, however, participation should be encouraged but not required; indeed, some students may opt to keep their contributions anonymous and that decision should be respected.

The topic of a crowdsourced poem is up to you. Options include allowing students to vote on a theme or choosing a discipline-specific concept or issue currently being explored in your class or program. When students are finished, debrief the process of creating a crowdsourced poem, focusing specifically on collaboration. Ask questions like: What were the benefits of co-authoring a poem? What were the challenges?

If you have the time and resources, consider recording the poem, adding music, and sharing the finished piece with your school or community organization.

Below is an example entitled *Love Without Violence* [Amor Sin Violencia], written by students in a first-year undergraduate seminar as part of a collaboration with a youth-centered Peruvian organization aimed at raising awareness about discrimination and gender-based violence. To keep the poem cohesive, students were given various sentence stems and instructed to contribute one to two lines. The lines were then compiled and organized into one poem and translated into Spanish. The English version is printed first followed by the Spanish-language version.

Example of crowdsourced poetry.
Printed with permission from the student authors.

Love Without Violence

> Love without violence is patience.
> It's having an open mind,
> And accepting others regardless of differences.
> No matter our differences, everyone deserves to be loved.
> Love without violence means offering kindness,
> Having compassion for everyone,
> And seeing the humanity in each person.
> It means peace without war.
> Love without violence is calm and affirming,
> Regardless of circumstance.
> It is pure and unconditional, steadfast and generous.
>> Like the love of a mother, it forgives, it fulfills, and it is always by your side.
> Love without violence is like ceviche, made up of abundant ingredients so flavorful they diminish the sting of hate.
> Love without violence is the feeling of golden sunlight,
> It is comforting, it warms your soul to the core.
> A lasting love cannot be based on violence.
> Real love never hides,

It thrives with no limit.
It is without malice and holds no grudges.

I will love without violence by being understanding and patient,
Expressing kindness, caring, and appreciation,
Offering compassion and support,
And ensuring that everyone feels valued,
Loved,
And accepted,
Without condition.
I will create a more loving and compassionate world by listening to those around me,
Being kind and considerate to others,
Seeing the good in everyone,
Appreciating that we all come from different walks of life,
And putting the needs of others before my own.

We need to strive for a world—void of violence—where everyone feels safe enough to express who they truly are.
For such a world we will fight,
With love,
Together.

Amor Sin Violencia

Amor sin violencia es paciencia.
Es tener una mente abierta,
Y aceptar a los demás sin darle importancia a las diferencias.
No importan nuestras diferencias, todos merecemos amor.
Amor sin violencia significa ofrecer la bondad.
Tener compasión para todos,
Y ver la humanidad en cada persona.

Significa paz sin guerra.
Amor sin violencia es tranquilidad y afirmación.
No le da importancia a las circunstancias.
Es puro y sin condiciones, constante y generoso,
Como el amor de una madre, te perdona, te llena, y siempre está a tu lado.
Amor sin violencia es como ceviche, compuesto de ingredientes abundantes, y la salsa del odio no tanto pique.
Amor sin violencia es la sensación del sol dorado
Es consolador, calienta tu alma.
Un amor duradero no puede estar basado en la violencia.
El amor verdadero nunca se tiene que esconder,
Prospera sin límites.
No tiene malicia ni guarda rencor.

Amaré sin violencia siendo comprensivo y paciente.
Expresando bondad, cariño, y agradecimiento,
Ofreciendo compasión y apoyo,
Asegurando que todos se sientan valorados,
Queridos,
Y aceptados,
Sin condición.
Crearé un mundo con más amor y compasión escuchando a los demás,
Siendo amable y considerada con todos,
Buscando lo positivo en cada persona,
Agradeciendo que todos estamos en diferentes caminos,
Y poniendo las necesidades de otros por delante de las mías.

Necesitamos luchar por un mundo—libre de violencia—donde todos se sientan lo suficientemente seguros para expresar quienes son en realidad.
Por este mundo lucharemos,
Con amor,
Juntos.

Crowdsourced Songs

Musically inclined students or those looking for an extra challenge will likely find value in developing a crowdsourced song, defined as a collection of thematic words or phrases submitted by multiple people to form a song. The same guidelines used for crowdsourced poetry apply with the added tasks of adding a chorus and a melody. Alternatively, students may opt to use an existing melody from a popular song and change the lyrics. Because engagement looks different for everyone, we encourage you to provide various options for participation, including writing, singing, and using or creating makeshift instruments.

Justice Is a Butterfly

We created this low-stakes, creativity-generating activity to engage students in the use of literary devices, specifically metaphors and similes. Start by drawing a table with two columns on the board or on a piece of chart paper. On the left column, instruct students to list program or course-related concepts. For example, if you teach science, you could include terms like water cycle, atom, and hypothesis. On the right column, ask students to list objects or things *not* associated with the program or course.

Next, divide students into small groups. Instruct groups to choose one word from the left column and one word from the right column and craft a simile or metaphor. For each word, students should come up with a list of descriptors using their senses (i.e., sight, touch, taste, smell, and hear). They will use their simile or metaphor and descriptors to create a poem.

Three student examples are included below.

POWER Is Human

Written by: student authors

A force that can both build and degrade.
It flares from within,
A fiery desire to lead, to control, to reach even higher.

Humans are a force to be reckoned with,
A mighty power that has developed greed.
Without checks and balances and separation of powers,
The world would crumble indeed.

It's a flame that can warm, bring light to the dark,
But unchecked it burns, leaving a mark.
With power comes choice, a test of the heart.
To use it for good, a true work of art.

In human hands, power's a fragile thing,
A gift to aid, to protect, to bring passion and hope to the world,
In ways both big and small,
For power, in the end, is a human call.

Ethics Are a Whiteboard

Written by: student authors

Ethics are a whiteboard
Moral principles to guide every action
Defining character and informing decisions
Varies from person to person, class to class
A whiteboard is impermanent,
written on and erased as needed,
A tool for conveying information
plagued by the residue of past ideations
Both are a blank slate, changed by time and convenience.

Life Is Like a Taco

Written by: Koi Hooker

Life is like a taco.
We all have different ingredients and flavors.
Whether we were made soft or hard, big or small.
Some of us are spicy, some of us are corny, and some of

> us can be a bit beefy.
> Any way we are made, we are still made of the same wrapping,
> And we are all tacos in the end.

Concluding Thoughts

We hope the activities outlined in this chapter will foster a more connected and trusting learning community and lay a foundation for authentic storytelling. In the next chapter, we'll explore a multitude of storytelling formats and review inspiring student examples. Let's go!

Questions for Extended Student Dialogue

- Which activity did you most enjoy?
- Which activity did you find most challenging?
- To what extent, if at all, did these activities shift your perception of storytelling?

Questions to Encourage Educator Self-Reflection

- What activity did you most enjoy facilitating?
- Which activity was the most challenging to facilitate?
- How did students respond to these activities?
- To what extent, if at all, did these activities shift your perception of storytelling?
- What other ways might you integrate storytelling practices into your classroom or community?

Reference

Kleon, A. (2014, April 29). A brief history of my newspaper blackout poems. *Austin Kleon.* https://austinkleon.com/2014/04/29/a-brief-history-of-my-newspaper-blackout-poems

4

From Spoken Word to Photography

Exploring Storytelling Formats

We often think of stories as existing primarily in books and oral traditions. But the possibilities for creating and delivering a story are vast and growing. Yes, many stories are found in literature *and* they also manifest in poetry, photography, music, visual art, podcasts, and the digital spaces we inhabit. In this chapter, we begin by introducing the concept of multimodality. We'll explore how multimodal storytelling can enhance teaching and learning across disciplines. Then, we'll explore specific storytelling formats that can be integrated into classroom and community spaces, including spoken word poetry, music, theater, visual art, photography, TEDx style talks, digital storytelling, and children's books. By embracing multimodality and experimenting with these diverse formats, students can tap into their creativity and connect with audiences in meaningful ways, as they develop essential communication and critical thinking skills.

Multimodal Storytelling

Multimodality involves combining different modes of communication—such as written or spoken language, images, sounds, movement, and digital media—to create richer and more nuanced stories. The Multimodal Storytelling Menu below breaks down the different modes and how they can be applied.

Multimodal Storytelling Menu

Mode	Description	Examples
Linguistic	The use of written or spoken language for communication	Poems, short stories, captions, speeches
Visual	The use of images, photographs, illustrations, or videos for expression	Illustrations, infographics, photos, paintings
Aural	The use of sound, music, or sound effects to create atmosphere or enhance emotion	Soundscapes, instrumental music, sound effects
Gestural	The use of movement, gesture, or body language to communicate meaning or emotion	Dance performances, pantomime, sign language
Spatial	The use of physical space or arrangement of elements to create meaning or impact	Museum exhibits, architecture, interior design
Digital	The use of digital technologies for creation, sharing, and interaction	Digital art, online archives, GIFs

Multimodal Storytelling in Action

In one school a group of students, ignited by a classmate's story about the process of "coming out," embark on a multimedia project exploring the history and ongoing fight for LGBTQIA+ rights in their community. They locate oral histories online and categorize them thematically around activism and resilience. They set their research to original music composed by a classmate, capturing the emotional highs and lows of the journey toward equality. Using archival photographs and news clips, they create

a documentary that educates and celebrates the diverse voices and experiences within the LGBTQIA+ community. The film is screened at a school assembly and local community center, sparking important conversations about acceptance, allyship, and the ongoing fight for LGBTQIA+ rights.

Another group of students, deeply affected by environmental racism, channel their outrage into an interactive website. They use GIS (geographic information systems) mapping tools to visually depict the disproportionate concentration of polluting industries in their predominantly Latinx neighborhood. They create infographics that illustrate the health disparities faced by residents, incorporating data from local health organizations and government reports. They also record oral histories of community members affected by pollution, weaving their narratives into the larger story of environmental injustice. The website becomes an advocacy tool, raising awareness and galvanizing community action. Students present their findings to local officials and even testify at a city council meeting, using their project to push for a policy change.

By embracing multimodality, students can express themselves in more vibrant, dynamic, and robust ways. They learn that storytelling is about finding the most authentic and impactful way to communicate their experiences and perspectives to others. Further, the process of creating these storytelling projects fosters a sense of political efficacy, as students witness how their stories have the power not only to inform and educate but also to inspire action and create real change in their community (Gonzalez et al., 2024). As they witness the impact their stories can have—sparking conversations, challenging norms, and even prompting tangible change within their communities—they begin to internalize the belief that their voices matter. This realization can ignite a lifelong passion for civic engagement, encouraging them to participate in the democratic process, advocate for causes they believe in, and work toward a more just and equitable society (Gonzalez et al., 2024).

Exploring Storytelling Formats

Now that we've established the power of multimodality, we'll explore a variety of storytelling formats and how they can be integrated in classrooms and communities. The table below provides a snapshot of the formats covered in this chapter, highlighting the specific modes—linguistic, aural, visual, spatial, gestural, and digital—that each one employs.

Storytelling Format	Modes
Spoken Word Poetry	Linguistic, Aural, Gestural (Digital if recorded or shared online)
Music	Aural, Linguistic, Digital (Gestural if performed live with dance or movement)
Visual Art	Visual, Spatial, Digital (Linguistic if text is incorporated in the artwork)
Theater	Linguistic, Gestural, Spatial, Aural (Digital if recorded or streamed, Visual for sets and costumes)
Photography and Photovoice	Visual, Spatial, Linguistic (if captions), Digital (Aural if part of multimedia or with audio narrative)
TEDx Style Talks	Linguistic, Aural, Gestural, Digital (Visual if presentations include visual aids like slides or videos)
Digital Storytelling	Digital, Visual, Aural, Linguistic, Spatial
Children's Books	Visual, Linguistic, Digital (if e-book), Aural (if read aloud), Gestural (if part of interactive or dramatic read-alouds)

 Teaching Tip:

Storytelling resources and experts are all around us. Collaborate with your school's library, theater or social justice club, debate coach, or music teacher to build a database of storytelling knowledge. Encourage students to share the many ways they engage in storytelling—you may be surprised!

Spoken Word Poetry

Broadly, spoken word is poetic performance art that uses rhythm, repetition, and creative word play to tell stories. Though spoken word poetry predates the written word, American spoken word was shaped by and popularized during the Harlem Renaissance and Civil Rights Movement of the 1960s to explore and create awareness about the beauty and struggle of Black life. Given its origins, spoken word poetry is often, though not always, used to raise public consciousness and call for social change.

Because spoken word poetry tends to emphasize performance, some students may be intimidated about exploring this format. Taking a scaffolded approach using the pre-writing and warm-up strategies suggested in the previous chapter and sharing examples of spoken word poetry, particularly ones performed by youth, will help mitigate students' initial hesitations.

Additional points to consider when teaching spoken word poetry in the classroom include length and delivery. Though there are no formal rules related to spoken word, poems tend to be under three minutes. When it comes to delivery, the most impactful spoken word performances are well-written and effectively executed. Careful attention should be paid to intonation and the use of rhetorical and literary devices. Spoken word poems, particularly those intended to create awareness about social justice issues, often appeal to emotion. Further, the use of literary devices such as metaphors, similes, rhyme, repetition, and alliteration are used to strengthen imagery, heighten emphasis, and connect with an audience.

Additional information and resources, including examples of youth spoken word poetry from the annual Brave New Voices Festival, can be found at youthspeaks.org.

Music

Analogous to spoken word poetry, music often emphasizes performance and self-expression. The various elements of music—including lyrics, melody, harmony, tempo, instruments, and performance dynamics—shape how musicians tell stories. While musical storytelling may not appeal to everyone, most of us connect with music in some way. Indeed, each of us has a

favorite song; we can likely all identify soundtracks that define certain moments in our lives.

Analyzing lyrics to identify storytelling arcs, sharing songs that have been impactful, and exploring the use of literary and rhetorical devices in songs are straightforward ways to introduce students to musical storytelling. Those who are especially musically inclined should also be afforded opportunities to explore this format.

> **Activity Spotlight: Lyric Analysis**
>
> Instruct students, either individually or in pairs, to choose a song with a story structure or assign one to them. Ask students to analyze the song's lyrics by responding to a series of prompts like the ones we've outlined below.
>
> ♦ What and/or who is the song about?
> ♦ What is the speaker feeling?
> ♦ How does the singer use metaphors, similes, and other literary devices to tell their story?
> ♦ What is the song's narrative arc?
>
> Some of our favorite songs to analyze with students include "Thunder" by Imagine Dragons, "Anti-Hero" by Taylor Swift, "Pray for Me" by The Weeknd and Kendrick Lamar, and "Coat of Many Colors" by Dolly Parton.

Theater

Theater is a blank slate; it's an opportunity for both the actor and the audience to embody different perspectives and imagine new ways of being. Theater grounded in social justice confronts complex social issues—often in ways that challenge or disrupt dominant narratives—generates dialogue, and inspires the public to take action. Students interested in this format should

be encouraged to develop and perform a monologue or work with fellow peers on a collaborative piece.

If you're interested in integrating theater into your classroom or community setting, Theater of the Oppressed (TO) is a thought-provoking and dynamic option (Boal, 1993). TO is a form of community-based theater that engages audience members, known as "spect-actors," in working together to overcome an unjust or oppressive situation. TO encompasses a variety of techniques to engage students in building community, tackling important social issues, and constructing collaborative stories. For example, a group of seventh grade students may opt to perform a short skit demonstrating the personal impact of name-calling. The audience members or "spect-actors" would be encouraged to intervene and suggest alternative, equity-centered responses.

Effective facilitation of TO requires practice and intentionality. If you're interested in learning more, there are an abundance of TO-related resources available online.

 Activity Spotlight: Louder Than Words

As the old adage goes, actions often speak louder than words. Depending on the format, body language can be an important part of the storytelling exchange. Use the prompts below—or come up with your own—to help students practice telling a story without using words:

- Imagine you are eating a sandwich. Eat the sandwich as if you had just experienced a tragedy. Eat the sandwich as if you had just won the lottery.
- Imagine you are a parent whose child arrived home way past curfew. Without saying a word, express your disappointment in them.
- Imagine you are being followed by zombies. Convince your peers they are in danger.

Visual Art

Throughout history, visual art—such as painting, drawing, and printmaking—has been used as a means through which to create awareness about injustice and call the public to action. Through powerful imagery and/or text, art can push us to consider an issue from a different perspective or help us visualize the world we'd like to see.

> **Teaching Tip:**
>
> Students who opt for less conventional storytelling methods, such as music or visual arts, should be encouraged to create an artist's statement, a description of their piece accompanied by an explanation of the meaning of their work, their inspiration, and their creation process. An artist's statement tends to be brief—several lines are typically sufficient—and written in first person.

Exploring and engaging with social justice issues through visual art in a classroom or community setting affords youth the opportunity to dig into their creative side while ensuring more artistically inclined students have a chance to shine. Not sure how to integrate arts into your classroom or community? Not to worry—art is not bound by rules. Get your hands on a variety of art supplies and see what your students come up with; you may be surprised! You may also consider soliciting the insights of local experts by inviting a local artist, art teacher, or media specialist as a guest speaker.

The two examples below, printed with the permission of *#PassTheMicYouth*, illustrate youth-created visual art pieces related to themes of liberation and resistance.

Face Forward
Rachel M. James

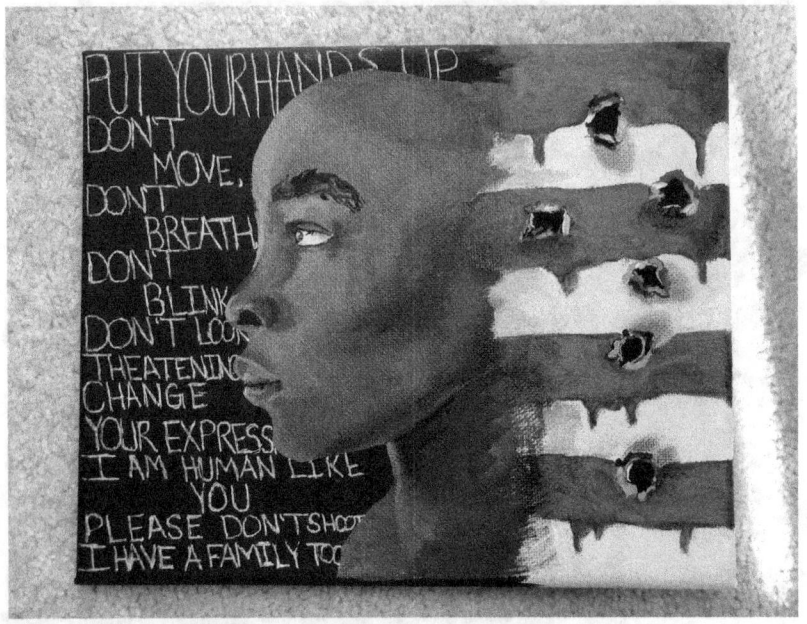

The text on this piece reads:

> Put your hands up.
> Don't move,
> Don't breathe,
> Don't look threatening.
> Change your expression.
> I am human like you.
> Please don't shoot.
> I have a family too.

Liberation of the Diaspora
Abigail Thomas

The text on this piece reads:

> I choose to shine now
> The ancestors of my past
> Led me to this life
> I won't disappoint
> My family heritage
> So I must fight now
> The future is soon
> Freedom is for everyone
> One diaspora.

Photography and PhotoVoice

Photography is a powerful medium through which to communicate stories, create public awareness, and amplify voices not

commonly heard in mainstream discourses. For example, the popular photo blog, *Humans of New York*, features a variety of thematic series that highlight the challenges and experiences faced by specific populations including inmates, refugees, and wounded veterans. Each series spotlights individual stories through the use of portraits and corresponding interview quotes.

PhotoVoice is a research methodology commonly used within classrooms and youth-serving organizations to help students identify issues within their school or community and determine possible solutions (Roberts et al., 2022). Students use the photographs to create public awareness about issue(s), engage in meaningful dialogue with peers and community members, and motivate individual and collective action.

 Teaching Tip:

Consider working with your school or community library to host a digital photo gallery exhibit of students' work. Invite school and community members to view the photographs and ask questions.

Students interested in using photography or PhotoVoice are encouraged to take and showcase a series of photographs and consider using captions to provide a more comprehensive snapshot of the issue(s) they are seeking to address.

In the example below, student Claudia Farnell used photography for a class assignment to tell a story about how racial and environmental disparities manifest in her city's local parks. Specifically, she compared a park in a relatively affluent, predominantly white neighborhood (Park #1) to a park in a working class, predominantly Black neighborhood (Park #2). The photographs illustrate clear differences regarding maintenance of the parks as

well as available amenities. The student used research to inform her story and substantiate her main points. She presented her final product to a group of her classmates, campus community members, and stakeholders, including the superintendent of the local office of parks and recreation. The presentation led to a series of productive conversations with parks and recreation and concrete steps to address the disparities.

PARK #1

PARK #2

PARK #1

PARK #2

PARK #1

PARK #2

TEDx Style Talks

Stories developed using a TEDx style format are structured around an idea—either an innovation or a familiar concept presented from a new angle. These talks, lasting between 5 and 18 minutes, are meant to provoke inquiry and generate dialogue. They should be solutions-driven and informed by credible sources. Because they focus on ideas, TEDx style talks are meant to appeal to a wide audience and should steer clear of rhetoric that may be divisive.

TEDx speaker guidelines and content guidelines are available online to assist students who may be interested in this format. TEDx events are independently organized so if you're feeling extra ambitious, work with students and colleagues to apply for a TEDxYouth license to organize a local event for and by young people in your school and community. Invite policymakers, elected officials, youth organizations, and other key community members to attend, making sure to factor in time for networking.

Whether hosting a TEDxYouth event or a general storytelling showcase, we always invite local community stakeholders to listen to and connect with young people. Such invitations have led to meetings, consultations, youth-community partnerships, and a wide array of additional opportunities for youth to expand the scope of their message in meaningful ways.

Digital Storytelling

Digital storytelling is an umbrella term to refer to technology-based narratives. Digital stories encompass a variety of multimedia formats such as podcasts, videos, and websites. Given youths' understanding of and interest in technology, digital storytelling is an effective format through which to engage students. If you're not particularly tech savvy, solicit the help of a librarian or multimedia specialist; they can provide support for identifying, accessing, and learning how to use the appropriate tools to meet all your digital storytelling needs.

Podcasts are a fun way to create and share digital stories in the classroom and on platforms like Spotify, Apple Podcasts, and Stitcher. Though podcasts are relatively easy to produce, a good podcast requires intentionality, the right equipment (even a phone and a quiet space will do!), and a script. That's right: Scripts prevent rambling, allow students to collect their thoughts, and considerably cut down on editing. Of course, the structure and level of detail in one's script depends largely on the style of the podcast. For example, a script for an interview-style podcast is less rigid to allow for improvisation and the organic flow of conversation.

Integrating music, ambient noise, audio clips, and interviews can make podcasts more engaging. The Youth Reporting Institute's curriculum (n.d.), cited at the end of this chapter, provides tools and strategies—including interview tips, script writing, and audio editing—for helping students develop podcasts. If you're interested in encouraging your students to write personal podcast-style stories related to science, check out The StoryCollider for resources and podcast episodes.

Let's not forget about social media. The vast majority of young people regularly use social media, both as content creators and consumers (Anderson et al., 2023). Encouraging students to create short and engaging social media videos about their topic allows them to leverage existing skills to create awareness about an issue they care about. Of course, not every young person uses social media so providing options is always a good idea.

Children's Books

Children's books tell a story using developmentally accessible words and images. Many children's books are intended to teach a lesson, often related to character education and celebrating differences. Children's books can also teach about complex social issues, from the local to the global, using simple language. Students, especially those with an interest in working with

children, may be particularly interested in this format. Digital tools like StoryJumper and My Storybook make it easy to write and illustrate children's books.

Below is an excerpt of a children's book, *Escape from Space*, created by an undergraduate student. Set in the future, the book follows the experiences of a grandmother whose family had to "escape to space" after the perils of climate change caused the earth to become uninhabitable. It is meant to warn about the implications of climate change and the need for sustainability and immediate action.

An excerpt from *Escape to Space*, written and illustrated by Hannah Jackson:

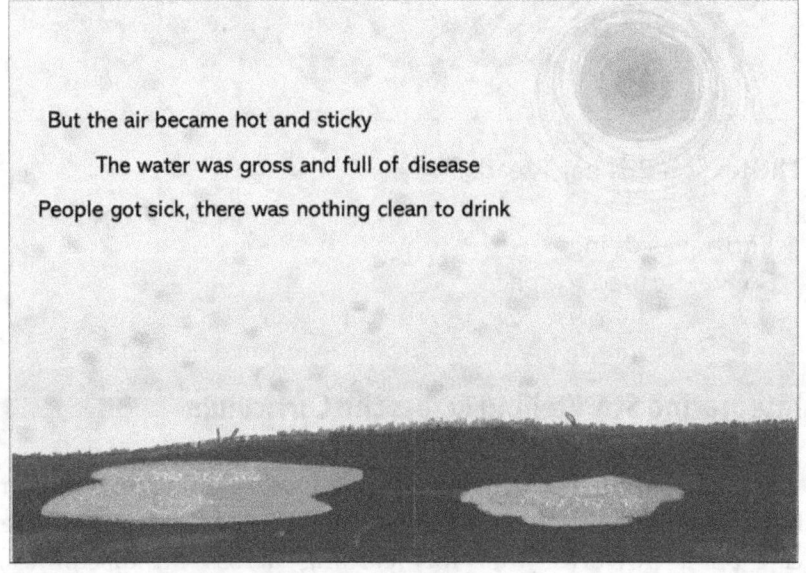

The text on this page reads:

> But the air became hot and sticky
> The water was gross and full of disease
> People got sick, there was nothing clean to drink

The text on this page reads:

Earth was dying
So we escaped to space

Integrating Storytelling Across the Curriculum

The skills students develop through storytelling extend far beyond language arts or social studies classrooms. Storytelling can be a powerful tool for learning across all disciplines, enriching understanding and fostering deeper engagement with the subject matter. Here's how educators in various subject and programmatic areas can leverage storytelling to enhance student learning:

History: Breathing Life into the Past

In history class, students can step into the shoes of historical figures and craft first-person narratives from their perspectives,

breathing life into the past and forging personal connections to historical events. For instance, during a unit on the Great Depression, students write letters from the perspective of a child living under dire conditions. They can draw upon primary source documents like photographs, newspaper articles, and oral histories from the Library of Congress to inform their narratives, gaining a deeper understanding of the emotional and social impact of this historical period. This approach aligns with the principles of *historical empathy*, which emphasizes the importance of understanding the past through the eyes of those who lived it (Barton & Levstik, 2004).

Science: Connecting Data to Lived Experience

Science classes and community-based programs offer a unique opportunity to blend personal narrative with scientific inquiry. For example, students can explore the local ecosystem by conducting field research on plant and animal life and collecting data on biodiversity, species interactions, and habitat conditions. Perhaps they remember a favorite childhood fishing spot that has changed over time, or they notice a decline in the population of a particular bird species they used to see frequently. By weaving together scientific data and personal stories, students create a more holistic and meaningful understanding of the natural world, recognizing the interconnectedness of scientific knowledge and cultural perspectives (Neeley et al., 2020). This approach aligns with *place-based education*, emphasizing the importance of connecting learning to the local environment and community (Sobel, 2004).

Math: Quantifying Everyday Experiences

Students can use storytelling to make math more relevant and meaningful by connecting it to their everyday lives. For example, students can create stories about using math to plan a budget for a family vacation, calculate the ingredients for a recipe, or design a scale model of their dream house. They can use data storytelling to explore social justice issues, such as analyzing statistics on income inequality in their community and then

collecting narratives from local newspapers or online forums to create a multi-layered narrative that combines quantitative data with personal stories. This approach reinforces mathematical concepts and cultivates critical thinking skills and a sense of social responsibility (Gutstein, 2006).

Arts: Expressing Identity

The arts provide a rich platform for personal storytelling and self-expression (Eisner, 2002). In dance class, students can choreograph pieces that explore their cultural heritage or personal experiences, using movement to convey emotions and ideas that may be difficult to articulate in words. In music class, they can compose songs that tell stories about their lives, communities, or the world around them, using melody, harmony, and rhythm to create a unique and personal expression. In visual arts, they create self-portraits that reflect their identities or use different media to illustrate stories from their lives or the lives of others.

 Teaching Tip:

To foster interdisciplinary connections through storytelling, encourage students to:

- connect different subjects through common themes like identity, community, or social justice;
- use diverse storytelling modes, including written narratives, oral histories, visual art, music, dance, and digital media;
- collaborate across disciplines, working with educators from other subject areas to create interdisciplinary projects that leverage the power of storytelling to enhance learning and engagement.

By weaving a variety of storytelling formats and multimodal expression into their respective subjects and program areas, educators can create richer and more engaging learning experiences. Students learn to see the world not as a series of isolated facts, but as interconnected narratives, each with its unique perspective and mode of expression. Whether they're stepping into the shoes of a historical figure, exploring the complexities of an ecosystem, or using data to tell a story about social justice, students develop critical reflection, empathy, and a deeper understanding of the subject matter. This approach equips them with the creative and analytical skills necessary to become lifelong learners, critical thinkers, and compassionate global citizens.

Concluding Thoughts

When it comes to storytelling, there is no shortage of dynamic modes and formats. We hope this exploration of multimodality and diverse storytelling approaches provides a multitude of useful options for engaging students in ways that leverage their unique interests and skills. In the next chapter, we'll explore practices for developing critical reflection, a crucial component for teaching and building informed social impact stories.

Questions for Extended Student Dialogue

- What storytelling format are you most interested in trying, and why?
- Which format do you feel most comfortable using to express yourself?
- What are some of the challenges you anticipate in using different storytelling formats?

- How can you use multimodality to enhance your storytelling and connect with your audience more effectively?
- How can different storytelling formats be used to address social issues and promote change?
- Is there a format not covered in this chapter that you would like to learn more about?

Questions to Encourage Educator Self-Reflection

- What storytelling format are you most interested in implementing with students, and why?
- Which format do you feel most comfortable teaching, and how can you build your confidence in using other formats?
- What are some of the challenges you anticipate in integrating multimodal storytelling into your curriculum?
- How can you create a supportive and inclusive classroom environment where students feel comfortable experimenting with different storytelling formats?
- With whom can you collaborate to enrich students' understanding and application of various storytelling formats and modes?

References

Anderson, M., Faverio, M., & Gottfried, J. (2023). *Teens, social media, and technology 2023*. Pew Internet & American Life Project.

Barton, K. C., & Levstik, L. S. (2004). *Teaching history for the common good*. Routledge.

Boal, A. (1993). *Theater of the oppressed*. Theater Communications Group.

Eisner, E. W. (2002). *The arts and the creation of mind*. Yale University Press.

Gonzalez, M., Kokozos, M., Byrd C., & McKee, K. (2024). Storytelling through a critical positive youth development framework: A mixed methods approach. *Journal of Youth Development, 19*(1), 2.

Gutstein, E. (2006). *Reading and writing the world with mathematics: Toward a pedagogy for social justice*. Routledge.

Neeley, L., Barker, E., Bayer, S. R., Maktoufi, R., Wu, K. J., & Zaringhalam, M. (2020). Linking scholarship and practice: Narrative and identity in science. *Frontiers in Communication, 5*, 35. https://doi.org/10.3389/fcomm.2020.00035

Roberts, L. T., Stein, C. H., & Tompsett, C. J. (2022). Youth views of community needs: A photovoice collaboration. *Children and Youth Services Review, 139*, 106563.

Sobel, D. (2004). *Place-based education: Connecting classrooms & communities*. Orion Society.

Youth Reporting Institute. (n.d.). *Youth reporting institute curriculum*. www.wunc.org/youth-radio/youth-reporting-institute-curriculum

5

Positionality, Power, and Privilege

Building Critical Reflection

Amelia and Priya are two students in a storytelling summer camp for high-achieving kids from across the county. As part of a series of icebreaker activities, one of the camp educators asks the group to create a collage of images that represent who they are. Both Priya and Amelia's mosaics include images of the sports they play.

Priya looks at Amelia's mosaic and says, "Why does your school get to have a swim team?"

"Doesn't your school?"

"No. We don't have a pool nearby."

"My school has a pool. The Boosters paid for it."

"Oh," Priya sighs. "That's because a bunch of rich kids go to your school."

"Or maybe they care more about their kids' education," Amelia counters.

Amelia and Priya are meeting for the first time at camp. As they share their collages, they're not only learning about each other but also beginning to explore how their identities shape their perspectives. They're discovering unexpected similarities and differences—and may find themselves wondering what these differences mean. With critical reflection, Amelia and Priya

can start to understand how who they are connects to broader social questions.

In the introduction, we emphasized the guiding principle that *critical reflection is a prerequisite for students and educators*. In Chapter 2, we emphasized the importance of us as educators developing our critical reflection. In this chapter we focus on developing students' critical reflection and explore how it supports social impact storytelling. We also provide activities for building critical reflection and show how these can contribute to students' sense of belonging.

Defining Critical Reflection

Critical reflection is an extension of critical thinking; it is a cyclical process of questioning, examining assumptions, and considering various perspectives in order to identify and analyze the social, political, and economic forces shaping individuals and communities. Critical reflection gives students an informed perspective from which to view social issues such as poverty, anti-LGBTQIA+ bullying, and access for people with disabilities. Instead of assuming that parents in Priya's neighborhood don't value education, for example, Amelia can think about the historical and economic factors that might limit their ability to raise money for their local school, or the factors that made it possible for the Boosters to raise money at her school. Here are three specific aspects of critical reflection to emphasize for students: positionality, privilege, and power dynamics. We'll provide more examples of teaching techniques in Chapter 8.

Positionality

Positionality describes our social location—the intersection of our race, gender, religion, sexual orientation, and national origin, among other identities—and our proximity to power and influence. Our positionality influences how we perceive the world and how we are perceived. The concept of intersectionality (Crenshaw, 2017) reminds us that two people who share one identity might have very different experiences because of their

other identities. Take Amelia and Priya, for example. They share their gender and age but have different kinds of sports available to them at school. While Priya is able to play kickball through her local Boys and Girls Club, Amelia's school hosts a swim team that can practice in their own pool.

Privilege

Privilege refers to unearned advantages and benefits that certain individuals or groups have based on their positionality (Johnson, 2018). Amelia benefits from the wealth of her parents and neighbors in ways that Priya cannot. While Priya's family and community also have strengths, these are less likely to be recognized and appreciated by schools and the broader society. In Chapter 6 we'll discuss the concept of community cultural wealth and how we as educators can honor the knowledge students bring into our community.

Power Dynamics

Because of privilege, different social groups hold power, and that power operates on a number of levels to influence our daily lives to the benefit of some groups at the expense of others. By understanding how the levels operate and intersect, we can better explain the whys behind social issues. We can think about four types of power: individual, institutional, economic, and cultural.

Individual Power is the ability an individual person has to act against another. For example, a white store clerk is exercising his power when he follows a Black youth around a store because he expects the youth to steal. As another example, a US-born business owner can refuse to hire immigrants to work at her business. These examples are forms of interpersonal prejudice and discrimination, but discrimination can occur at other levels as well.

Institutional Power is the ability of organizations or established systems to influence behavior and decision-making through formal structures, rules, and enforcement mechanisms. When a school principal sets rules as expectations, that is power over an educational institution. The government is another institution that can set laws and policies that might discriminate.

Economic Power is the influence or control over resources, production, and distribution of goods and services. This can

be wielded by individuals, corporations, or institutions. For example, wealthy donors can use their individual economic power to influence political decisions. The gaps between rich and poor neighborhoods, like Amelia and Priya are noticing, is another form of economic power. In their case, the economic power allows one school to fund more expensive sports.

Cultural Power is the ability to shape norms, values, beliefs, and behaviors through influence over media, education, and social institutions. This can lead to the dominance of certain perspectives and marginalization of others. Media-driven cultural influence can be seen in the dominance of certain beauty standards, which can be enforced in many different ways. The pressure to conform to beauty standards and gender roles more generally is another example of cultural power. Amelia and Priya might notice that others assume the swim team is more competitive and prestigious than kickball, when both girls have to work hard and demonstrate similar levels of teamwork.

In sum, critical reflection requires students to look inward, examining how their lived experiences and social identities shape the lens through which they view the world. They must appreciate their positionality and the privileges it may give them and analyze the power dynamics within their experiences and society more broadly to understand and act on the social issues they care about. As demonstrated in the reinforcing arrows in our CPYD model (see the introduction), critical reflection can drive critical action that then supports supportive environments for continued critical reflection. Through understanding the root causes of social issues, students will be better able to think about effective solutions both for their local contexts and their broader communities. With their expanded understanding, Priya and Amelia could work together to advocate for equitable school funding.

Critical Reflection and Storytelling

Storytelling offers students the chance to feel that their lived experiences are valued and appreciated, especially those from marginalized backgrounds whose experiences often go

unrecognized (Borrero et al., 2022). It empowers them to raise awareness about social issues, build solidarity across diverse groups, and drive social change (Berrett-Abebe et al., 2023; Miller et al., 2020). Through critically grounded storytelling, students connect their personal narratives to a broader understanding of power, positionality, privilege, and oppression (Aldana et al., 2016; Bell, 2019). In particular, counternarratives—an account of events told from the perspective of someone who has been historically marginalized, oppressed, excluded, or silenced—allow young people to challenge the status quo, promote social change by disrupting entrenched beliefs and encourage more equitable and inclusive perspectives both in the classroom and beyond (Miller et al., 2020; Solórzano & Yosso, 2002). (For more on counternarratives, see Chapter 9.)

Ultimately, critical reflection enables students to tell authentic, powerful stories that drive social change. In our research (Gonzalez et al., 2024), we followed 14 students engaged in a storytelling curriculum grounded in our CPYD framework. Opportunities for storytelling helped these students gain a stronger awareness of their positionality and a deeper understanding of social justice concepts. This transformative effect was clear in their reflections: One student shared that storytelling deepened her understanding of inequality by exposing her to others' struggles, while another noted that these narratives inspired her to be a better ally and advocate for change. Storytelling thus fosters critical reflection that not only raises awareness but also motivates actionable steps toward a more inclusive world (Ball, 2018; Solórzano & Yosso, 2002).

Developing Critical Reflection

So how can we use storytelling to support students' critical reflection? We ask students to acknowledge their social identities, notice patterns across identities, appreciate intersectionality, understand privilege and oppression, and feel motivated to take action.

Acknowledge positionality. Asking students to acknowledge their location within their multiple social identities helps them see how the groups we belong to influence our perspectives and how we interact with the world. Recognizing their unique position allows students to understand why it's important for others to hear their stories. While others may share some of their experiences, no one experiences the world exactly as they do.

Acknowledging positionality also helps students gain a better sense of how their peers might view the world based on *their* social locations and why it's important to share different perspectives. By recognizing their social locations based on socioeconomic status, Priya and Amelia begin to recognize how financial resources influence the opportunities available to them. This recognition can motivate them to inform others.

 Activity Spotlight: Identity Mosaic

Define social identities as our identities related to social identity groups we belong to (e.g., race, gender, and religion) and personal identities as how we see ourselves as individuals. Give students a few minutes to list words that come to mind when they think about their personal and social identities.

Next, ask students to spend 20 minutes creating an identity mosaic by collecting images and/or photographs that represent their personal identities (i.e., aspects of their personality, career aspirations, hobbies, values, etc.) and social identities. Mosaics can be created digitally (i.e., in Canva or using slides) or on construction paper using magazine clippings.

Encourage students to share their identity mosaics if they feel comfortable. Some students may not if their mosaics reflect aspects of their identity that they feel vulnerable about. Even if students don't share, they can discuss with their partner what it felt like to create the mosaic and how they decided what to represent. Prompt students

to make connections as to how the various facets of their social identities are meaningful and yet complex by asking:

- In what ways are these facets of identity meaningful and important to you?
- What roles do institutions, such as schools or places of worship, play in shaping your identities?
- Consider the choices you made in determining which identities to display. What did you choose to convey and why?

We tend to pay less attention to the identities where we hold privilege, so activities where we label our social identities can be important for challenging the assumption that our identities don't affect us or that only "other" groups have a distinct culture. Amelia may not have questioned whether high schools should have pools before she talked with Priya during the mosaic activity.

The act of labeling can be empowering for some students because it provides a positive answer to one of the questions of belonging we saw back in Chapter 2: "Does anyone here even notice me?" (see Walton & Brady, 2017). Labeling helps us affirm students' sense of belonging because the student is seen as a member of a particular group and yet still accepted as part of the larger classroom community. For example, one of our students has Native American heritage that often goes unrecognized because of her name and appearance. For her, it's important that her peers know and value her background.

While activities like the identity mosaic can empower students by helping them feel noticed and valued, some may not be ready to share certain aspects of their backgrounds, especially if those identities make them feel vulnerable or carry a risk of misunderstanding or judgment from peers. To create a supportive environment for exploring social identities, it's important to recognize that students may still feel pressure to disclose parts of their identity, even if we're not explicitly asking

them to share. One way to minimize this pressure is to give students the option to select which identities to highlight and offer alternative ways to participate, such as reflecting privately in a journal or discussing their identities in general terms without specific labels. Educators can also normalize a range of choices by acknowledging upfront that everyone's comfort with sharing will vary and that it's equally valid to focus on identities they feel safe sharing. Maintaining a choice-based, flexible approach is also consistent with UDL (Universal Design for Learning) and the principles of privacy and caring that we discussed in previous chapters. To further support this environment, educators should be attentive to any signals of discomfort and be ready to provide reassurance or an option to opt out.

 Activity Spotlight: Definition Gallery

- Write key terms on chart paper, one term per page:
  - Social Identities
  - Stereotype
  - Discrimination
  - Privilege
  - Oppression
- Hang the terms in around the room, creating five stations.
- Assign participants into five teams. Each team should begin at a different station. At each station, teams should write down words, phrases, and/or examples they associate with the assigned term.
- After one minute, groups rotate until each group has visited all five stations, underscoring or adding to previous responses.
- Once all stations have been visited, instruct participants to return to their first station and read all the responses aloud to the group.
- Based on the responses, work with participants to generate a collective definition for each term. You can use the definitions below as a guide:

- **Social identities:** The aspects of our identities based on social identity groups to which we belong, such as gender, race, and sexual orientation. Social identities can be self-claimed and/or ascribed, fluid, and context-based and can change over time.
- **Stereotype:** A pervasive, oversimplified attitude, assumption, or belief about a specific group.
- **Discrimination:** Prejudicial actions, both conscious and unconscious, based on an individual's actual or perceived social identity group membership.
- **Privilege:** Unearned access to resources and unfair advantages afforded to individuals based solely on social identity group membership. Privilege can be reaped or exploited unfairly, knowingly or unknowingly.
- **Oppression:** The combination of prejudice and institutional power that results in a system that maintains advantage and disadvantage based on social identity group memberships across interpersonal, institutional, and sociocultural levels.

♦ Reflect by asking questions such as:
- What was it like to engage in this activity? What terms were new for you? What terms, if any, do you still have questions about?
- What was beneficial about working together to generate collective definitions of these terms?
- In what ways are these terms related?
- How do your life experiences impact your understanding of these terms?
- How and to what extent will having an understanding of these terms shape your engagement with storytelling for social change?

This activity was adapted with permission from Amplifying Youth Voices: A Social Change Curriculum *by* #PassTheMicYouth

Notice patterns across identities. When students like Amelia and Priya pay attention to social identities, they begin to see patterns—common experiences or challenges shared by individuals from the same group. We as educators can label patterns with terms like "privilege" and "oppression" and call attention to the implications of these patterns. For example, we can ask students to think about which high schools in their county are better funded and what that means not only for individual students, but for the county as a whole. Later, we'll encourage students to think about why those funding disparities exist and point them to power dynamics.

Storytelling is especially effective for illuminating these patterns because it allows the storyteller to craft a narrative that emphasizes recurring experiences related to social issues. Through literary devices like metaphors and repetition (see Chapter 4), stories can tap into our brain's natural tendency to recognize and anticipate patterns. This makes storytelling a powerful way to draw connections and prompt critical reflection, encouraging listeners to consider not just individual experiences, but the systemic issues underlying them. In critically grounded storytelling, this pattern recognition can even serve as a call to action, inspiring students to consider how they might address these shared challenges in their communities.

Appreciate intersectionality. Some of the patterns students notice may correspond to stereotypes, such as boys liking sports more than girls. Even still, we can help students realize that each person expresses their social identities in unique ways. We can also introduce the concept of intersectionality and encourage students to consider how various aspects of their identities—race, class, gender, ability—interact to shape their lived experiences in complex ways. Priya and Amelia can think about how the cultures of their families influenced which sports they enjoy, whether it's cricket or lacrosse. And they can both appreciate the international appeal of soccer. This aspect of critical reflection in particular can build empathy, challenge assumptions, and help them appreciate diverse perspectives. With these skills, students craft more compelling social impact stories, ones that acknowledge the complexity of individuals within groups.

Understand privilege and oppression. Once students have an awareness of patterns related to social identity, they can begin to gain a greater understanding of how privilege and oppression operate in society on a systemic level. We can talk to students like Amelia and Priya about historical policies like redlining that made it easier for white families to own homes in certain neighborhoods and build generational wealth. The students can analyze each level of power to identify the complexities and appreciate their positionality within them. We should also encourage students to explore why inequality exists and persists despite efforts to address it.

Furthermore, because we all have multiple intersecting social identities, we may experience privilege in some settings and situations and marginalization in others. While Priya may have disadvantages because of her socioeconomic status, at school she experiences privilege compared to her immigrant peers because she was born in the United States. As educators, we can guide students in recognizing these complexities.

It's important to give students clear definitions for social justice terms and to clarify the mechanisms of privilege and oppression. However, especially at early stages, we don't want to let the abstract and conceptual overwhelm students or distract them from the ultimate goal of telling authentic, personal stories. Social justice reveals itself in the everyday, so by meeting students where they are and carefully scaffolding these concepts, we can build up to a deeper understanding.

When students understand the systemic nature of privilege and oppression, they can weave more nuanced perspectives into their storytelling, showing how individual experiences are shaped by societal forces. For example, students like Amelia and Priya might explore how historical policies like redlining continue to impact their communities today, affecting access to resources like quality schools and housing. This understanding allows students to tell stories that not only reflect their personal journeys but also highlight the broader social contexts that influence their lives.

Recognizing the complexities of privilege and oppression also allows students to create multidimensional characters and

narratives. By exploring how people can experience privilege in some settings and marginalization in others, students can construct stories that reflect the intersecting and sometimes contradictory aspects of identity. For instance, Priya might write a story that reflects her socioeconomic challenges but also acknowledges her relative privilege as a US-born student compared to her immigrant peers. This depth enriches storytelling, fostering empathy and a greater awareness of how power and positionality influence people's experiences.

Feel motivated to take action. After understanding privilege and oppression, students can be motivated to take action toward social change. Educators can foster this motivation by providing opportunities for students to engage in advocacy, activism, or community service. Whether it's writing letters to policymakers, participating in local community initiatives, or creating awareness campaigns on social media, students should be encouraged to translate their critical reflection into real-world impact. We'll discuss more opportunities to support action in Chapter 11. Social impact stories often propose solutions to social issues and inspire the audience to take action.

Create a sense of belonging. Activities like the identity mosaic not only help build critical reflection, they can help students get to know each other and build trust, community, and connection (see Chapter 2). Because they've shared mosaics, Priya and Amelia can now bond over their shared love of sports and use that as a foundation to explore their different experiences in their neighborhoods. They can use their knowledge of intersectionality to be interested in how their experiences in sports might be similar and different. They'll use their understanding of privilege and oppression to notice unfair policies and be able to craft social impact stories that they can use to promote equity in funding across the county.

Returning to the questions of belonging we saw in Chapter 2 (Walton & Brady, 2017), critical reflection offers affirmative answers to a number of them. In particular, students will see that the question, "Are people like me incompatible with this setting or behavior?" depends on many social, political, and historical factors. They also start to consider how they can work to make

their communities a place for all to belong, starting with your community space or classroom.

Navigating Resistance and Emotional Labor

In any classroom focused on social justice and equity, resistance is inevitable. As they learn more about oppression, students may feel overwhelmed by the complexities of social systems and their roles within these systems. Those with privilege may interpret discussions about inequality as personal attacks and feel guilt or defensiveness. These feelings can lead to some students shutting down, dismissing the material, or becoming argumentative. It's important to recognize that this is a common reaction and a natural part of the learning process (Byrd, 2023; Byrd et al., 2020). By building a trusted and connected community (see Chapter 2), you can create a space where students can work through these emotions while remaining accountable to the work of social change.

Remember that it can be difficult to make sense of the ways in which we are privileged because we often don't notice our unearned advantages. For example, Amelia will fairly insist that her parents worked hard to give her a middle-class lifestyle. It's important to acknowledge that individual efforts *do* matter in outcomes. At the same time, white families in the US have benefitted from policies that have made it easier for them, compared to people of color, to own their own homes, live in safe neighborhoods, and be employed in high-paying jobs (Johnson, 2018).

For students of color, LGBTQIA+ students, and students from other marginalized backgrounds, the emotional labor can be particularly heavy when discussing social issues (Mildred & Zúñiga, 2004; Rodriguez, 2009). Many of these students are already acutely aware of how privilege and oppression shape their lives, and they may feel frustrated when their peers with privilege are just beginning to understand these dynamics. They may also feel pressure to educate others about their lived experiences. It's vital for educators to acknowledge this emotional labor and

to avoid placing the responsibility of teaching about inequality on students with marginalized identities. Providing spaces where these students can process their emotions and share their experiences on their terms—without being expected to represent their entire group—can help alleviate some of this pressure.

At the same time, students from marginalized backgrounds often desire recognition for the extra emotional and intellectual labor they are doing. These students may feel frustrated when their contributions go unnoticed or when their experiences are dismissed or minimized. Educators must be intentional in validating and valuing their perspectives, ensuring that these students feel seen and respected.

Another concern for students from marginalized backgrounds is that they may have internalized negative messages and stereotypes about their group, messages that may reveal themselves in the students' sense of self-worth and in the stories they tell about themselves. As educators, we can carefully challenge these beliefs through teaching critical reflection—we've found teaching counternarratives, discussed in Chapter 8, to be particularly effective. In our research discussed earlier (Gonzalez et al., 2024), one student shared how she was able to "unlearn" the habit of "feeling embarrassed by [her] identity and culture" (p. 7). Activities like caucus groups, described below, can help students process emotions specific to their group identity with peers who share that identity.

 Activity Spotlight: Peer Reflection

Caucus groups, also called affinity groups, provide students the opportunity to reflect and process within identity groups before coming back to share with the larger community. For more on caucus groups, check out the guide by the Interaction Institute for Social Change (2023) in the references. In-depth caucus groups can be a high-risk activity, so you may want to seek additional training before facilitating them. Here is a pair version that may be lower stakes for students.

- **Introduction:** Begin by explaining the purpose of caucus groups to the class. Note that we can identify with others based on a variety of social identities—race, gender, religion, or even which part of town you grew up in. Emphasize to students that they can choose based on the group they feel most connected to, regardless of how others might see them or what others want them to identify with. You can also ask students to pair up based on common interests or hobbies.
- **Pair Discussions:** Ask students to select a partner who they feel is most similar to them. Remind students about the definition of social identities and ask them to discuss their shared experiences based on an identity they share. Remind students about the community agreements regarding confidentiality and let them know they may want to keep some parts of their discussion within the pair. Have students reflect on questions such as:
    - How do your identities shape your experience in this class?
    - What challenges have you faced because of your identity?
    - What strengths do you feel come from it?
    - What do you wish others understood about your experiences?
- Within the pairs, encourage students to consider how multiple aspects of their identity (e.g., being a first-generation college student and Latina, or being queer and working-class) may intersect, and remind them that their experiences may differ from their partner.
- **Whole Group Discussion:** After the pair discussions, invite students to share insights or reflections with the larger group. Some students may feel comfortable speaking, while others may prefer to

> observe. Ensure that sharing is voluntary, and recognize the value of both speaking and listening.
>
> Caucus groups give students a space to reflect in a supportive, identity-affirming environment before opening up to the broader class. By allowing them to connect with peers who share similar experiences, they can feel validated and understood. Then, bringing the conversation back to the whole class encourages cross-group learning and helps build a more inclusive and knowledgeable community.

Finally, it's important to recognize that this work can be exhausting for everyone. Talking about privilege and oppression often brings up deep-seated emotions, and many students may feel tired, upset, or discouraged. As educators, it's crucial to check in with students and remind them that discomfort is part of growth. At the same time, pacing the lessons and allowing time for reflection and self-care can help prevent burnout. Think about helping students make self-care plans and be sure to take time for yourself also. When done well, this process can build resilience, empathy, and a strong commitment to social change.

Concluding Thoughts

Critical reflection is the foundation of telling nuanced, authentic social impact stories. Through recognizing their positionality, the power dynamics in society, and the ways privilege and oppression influence their experiences, young storytellers are better able to craft narratives that reveal, challenge, and inspire. This might seem like a tall order for students, but in the next chapter we'll describe examples of young people's impact in society and show how you can create a student-centered classroom or community organization that creates a sense of agency and empowerment.

Questions for Extended Student Dialogue

- What aspects of your identity do you think are most visible to others, and which ones are less noticeable? How does this impact how you move through different spaces?
- Can you think of a time when someone made an assumption about you based on one of your social identities? How did that affect you?
- How do different aspects of your identity (e.g., race, gender, class) interact to shape your experiences? Can you think of a situation where one aspect of your identity was more prominent than another?
- Why is it important to understand that identities are complex and intersect in unique ways? How can this understanding help us create more inclusive spaces?
- Why is critical reflection an important aspect of social impact storytelling?
- How does noticing patterns across identities and acknowledging intersectionality allow us to tell more nuanced and authentic stories?
- How can social impact stories motivate others to take action?
- Why is learning critical reflection so emotionally taxing? What can you do to take care of yourself?

Questions to Encourage Educator Self-Reflection

- How have your social identities shaped your understanding of privilege and oppression? Are there aspects of your privilege that you've had to confront or become more aware of in recent years?
- How do your social identities influence the way you teach and interact with your students? Are there

blind spots in how you relate to certain identities in your classroom?
- How would you respond to resistance or defensiveness from students with privilege? How can you approach these situations with empathy while still holding students accountable for their growth?
- How do you acknowledge and validate the emotional labor of marginalized students without placing the burden of education on them? What steps do you take to ensure they feel supported in your classroom?
- How do you care for yourself while navigating difficult conversations around privilege, oppression, and social justice? How do you maintain a constructive and safe learning environment for all students?
- How do you ensure that critical reflection in your classroom leads to meaningful action and change, rather than staying at the level of intellectual understanding?
- How do you create a balance between pushing students to confront difficult truths and providing them space to process their emotions? How do you gauge when students are ready to move from discomfort to action?
- How can you encourage students to craft social impact stories that reflect the complexity of positionality, privilege, and power?

References

Aldana, A., Richards-Schuster, K., & Checkoway, B. (2016). Dialogic pedagogy for youth participatory action research: Facilitation of an intergroup empowerment program. *Social Work with Groups, 39*(4), 339–358. https://doi.org/10.1080/01609513.2015.1076370

Ball, A. F. (2018). The power of stories: Storytelling as a tool for social justice education. In D. J. Clandinin & J. Hussein (Eds.), *Handbook of narrative inquiry: Mapping a methodology* (pp. 417–436). Sage.

Bell, L. A. (2019). *Storytelling for social justice: Connecting narrative and the arts in antiracist teaching* (2nd ed.). Routledge.

Berrett-Abebe, J., Reed, S. C., & Storms, S. B. (2023). Counternarratives: An antiracist approach in social work education, practice, and research. *Social Work, 68*(2), 122–130. https://doi.org/10.1093/sw/swad009

Borrero, N., Yeh, C. J., Dela Cruz, G., & Collins, T. (2022). The COVID-19 pandemic and emerging cultural assets. *Equity & Excellence in Education, 55*(4), 328–341. https://doi.org/10.1080/10665684.2021.1992603

Byrd, C. M. (2023). Cycles of development in learning about identities, diversity, and equity. *Cultural Diversity and Ethnic Minority Psychology, 29*(1), 43.

Byrd, C. M., Rastogi, R., & Elliot, E. R. (2020). Engagement with diversity experiences: A self-regulated learning perspective. In L. Parson & C. Ozaki (Eds.), *Teaching and learning for social justice and equity in higher education: Foundations* (pp. 137–156). Palgrave Macmillan.

Crenshaw, K. W. (2017). *On intersectionality: Essential writings*. The New Press.

Gonzalez, M., Kokozos, M., McKee, K., & Byrd, C. (2024). Storytelling through a Critical Positive Youth Development framework: A mixed methods approach. *Journal of Youth Development, 19*(1), 2.

Interaction Institute for Social Change. (2023, April 12). *Racial affinity group field guide*. IISC. https://interactioninstitute.org/racial-affinity-group-field-guide

Johnson, A. G. (2018). *Privilege, power, and difference*. McGraw Hill.

Mildred, J., & Zúñiga, X. (2004). Working with resistance to diversity issues in the classroom: Lessons from teacher training and multicultural education. *Smith College Studies in Social Work, 74*(2), 359–375. https://doi.org/10.1080/00377310409517721

Miller, R., Liu, K., & Ball, A. F. (2020). Critical counter-narrative as transformative methodology for educational equity. *Review of Research in Education, 44*(1), 287–313. https://doi.org/10.3102/0091732X20908501

Rodriguez, D. (2009). The usual suspect: Negotiating white student resistance and teacher authority in a predominantly white classroom. *Cultural Studies ↔ Critical Methodologies*, *9*(4), 483–508. https://doi.org/10.1177/1532708608321504

Solórzano, D. G., & Yosso, T. J. (2002). Critical race methodology: Counter-storytelling as an analytical framework for education research. *Qualitative Inquiry*, *8*(1), 23–44. https://doi.org/10.1177/107780040200800103

Walton, G. M., & Brady, S. T. (2017). The many questions of belonging. In A. J. Elliot, C. S. Dweck & D. S. Yaeger (Eds.), *Handbook of competence and motivation: Theory and application* (2nd ed., pp. 272–293). Guildford Press.

6

Centering Youth in Social Change Narratives

Jada never considered herself a "science person." For years, she associated science with complex formulas, abstract concepts, and old white guys in lab coats—their hair in a constant state of disarray. Aside from school, science didn't seem to have any bearing on Jada's daily life. Still, she dutifully learned the formulas, memorized the definitions, and did what was needed to get by.

Then Jada stepped into Ms. Urieta's classroom, a space endearingly designated "the idea lab." In Ms. Urieta's idea lab, students were encouraged to share their insights and experiences, ask questions, and provide feedback for shaping and improving assignments and class projects. The walls of Ms. Urieta's idea lab were adorned with field-shaping scientists and youth climate activists like Xiuhtezcatl Martinez, Greta Thunberg, and Vanessa Nakate who reflected the diverse backgrounds and interests of her students, including Jada.

Ms. Urieta wasn't limited by the mundane facts and abstract figures of a textbook. No. She connected scientific concepts like environmental sustainability to local, community-driven and youth-led initiatives like efforts to increase composting, reduce food waste, and build school and urban gardens.

Ms. Urieta's class projects focused on real-world issues that impacted local communities and her students always took center stage.

"How can we use science to reduce our school's energy consumption?" Ms. Urieta would ask, "How can science help us build more sustainable communities? How can you, as a scientist, student, and community member contribute to a more equitable and sustainable future?"

Ms. Urieta transformed the way students perceived, connected to, and interacted with science. For Jada, science was no longer just a subject to study; it was a tool for strengthening her community and building a better future.

Centering youth in social change narratives begins with centering students in the classroom and within youth-serving organizations—giving them a platform, as Ms. Urieta did, to ask questions, exchange ideas, and share experiences. A student-centered classroom operates under the belief that any work for and about young people must actively involve them in ways that are meaningful, bidirectional, and strengths-based.

Like Jada, students who feel like their perspectives have value and are meaningfully included in decision-making processes are more likely to view themselves as leaders and agents of social change (Ginwright & Cammarota, 2007; Gonzalez & Kokozos, 2019). Young people also thrive socially, emotionally, and academically when they feel empowered to participate in social change initiatives, particularly when their efforts are supported and valued by educators and other trusted adults (Ballard & Ozer, 2016; Lerner et al., 2005). For example, when we solicit and incorporate their feedback on school policies and protocols, like those related to bullying and the dress code, we signal to students that their ideas and experiences are valued and taken seriously. And because civically engaged young people are likely to become civically engaged adults (Arnold & Gagnon, 2020; Gonzalez et al., 2020), the benefits of youth leadership last a lifetime and resonate throughout schools, communities, and the world.

So what can we, as educators, do to center student voices and unlock the power and promise of young people's capacity to lead on the issues they most care about? In this chapter, we will review and apply practices for cultivating a student-centered, culturally sustaining classroom or community program—one

that lifts up the stories of young changemakers, past and present, and encourages student-led, adult-supported engagement.

Building Culturally Sustaining Classrooms and Communities

In the pursuit of creating classrooms and communities that center students—their histories, their voices, their perspectives—we, like Ms. Urieta, embrace practices that uplift students' unique experiences and nurture their diverse cultural and linguistic identities. We are inspired by culturally sustaining pedagogy (CSP), which aims to foster and preserve cultural pluralism, actively embracing, incorporating, and *sustaining* students' cultural identities in the classroom and within youth-serving organizations (Paris, 2012). By incorporating students' family traditions, home languages, and knowledge into the curriculum, we create spaces where students' identities are affirmed, their experiences are uplifted, and their agency is nurtured—ultimately fostering an environment that invites them to build and share authentic and meaningful stories. In this section, we will further examine CSP by focusing on two key concepts: funds of knowledge (Moll et al., 1992) and Bishop's mirrors, windows, and sliding glass doors metaphor (1990).

Funds of Knowledge: Recognizing Students' Cultural Wealth

A key concept within CSP is the idea of "funds of knowledge" (Moll et al., 1992). Funds of knowledge refers to the rich body of knowledge, skills, and experiences that students acquire through their families, communities, and cultural traditions. This knowledge is often overlooked or devalued in traditional educational settings, but CSP recognizes it as a valuable resource for learning. For example, a youth programming coordinator facilitating a nutrition-related program could invite students to share stories about food traditions in their families or communities. These stories might include recipes passed down through generations, special meals prepared for cultural celebrations, or memories of family gatherings centered around food. By tapping into these funds of knowledge through storytelling, the coordinator

enriches the program's curriculum and empowers students by recognizing their expertise and the cultural significance of food in their lives. This intentional integration of students' lived experiences and cultural knowledge into the learning environment extends beyond curriculum content; it also fosters a sense of community and belonging among participants.

 Teaching Tip:

While encouraging students to share family recipes and cultural traditions can be a valuable way to tap into their funds of knowledge, it's important to proceed with caution and sensitivity. Not all students may positively associate with family traditions or be comfortable disclosing them. Encourage students to share without feeling pressured to do so. Offer alternative ways for students to participate, such as researching and sharing cultural food traditions from countries outside the US.

Mirrors, Windows, and Sliding Glass Doors

The metaphor of mirrors, windows, and sliding glass doors (Bishop, 1990) is a helpful framework for understanding how curriculum and pedagogy can create inclusive and empowering learning environments. Mirrors reflect students' identities, windows offer glimpses into the wider world, and sliding glass doors allow them to engage with their communities.

In a high school literature classroom, for instance, the walls adorned with quotes from diverse authors and poets can act as mirrors, reflecting the myriad identities of the students within. A young Asian American student might see themselves in the words of Ocean Vuong, while a non-binary student might find resonance in the poetry of Andrea Gibson. These textual representations validate students' experiences and empower them to see themselves as part of a rich literary tradition.

The same classroom can also offer windows into worlds beyond students' immediate experiences. A unit on dystopian

fiction, for instance, could feature stories from marginalized communities, allowing students to understand the lived realities and struggles of those who are often silenced or overlooked. By engaging with these diverse narratives, students broaden their understanding of the world and develop empathy for those whose experiences differ from their own.

But mirrors and windows alone are not enough. Students need opportunities to step through the "sliding glass door" and engage with the world beyond the classroom. This could involve participating in community writing workshops, attending literary festivals, or interviewing local authors. For example, a class studying the Harlem Renaissance could visit a local museum or cultural center to learn about the artists, writers, and musicians who shaped this pivotal moment in African American history. This experiential learning deepens students' understanding of the curriculum and fosters a sense of agency and empowerment.

By intentionally incorporating mirrors, windows, and sliding glass doors into their classrooms, we can create learning environments that are not only culturally responsive but also politically engaging. We can empower students to see themselves as part of a larger literary and social context, connect with diverse perspectives, and use their voices to contribute to the ongoing conversation of literature and social change. This is the essence of political efficacy, the belief that one has the power to influence political and social processes (Gonzalez et al., 2024). And it is through this sense of agency that students are most likely to become engaged citizens who are committed to using their voices to create a more just and equitable world.

From Youth Representation to Youth-Led Action

Now that we know how to integrate student-centered, culturally sustaining practices into our classrooms and community organizations, let's explore three interconnected pillars that are essential for centering youth in social change narratives: recognizing the historical and contemporary impacts of youth

changemakers; amplifying youth voices through curriculum and representation; and fostering positive and productive youth–adult partnerships.

Recognizing Youth's Historical and Contemporary Social Change Impacts

Think back to when you were in middle and high school. How were children and youth positioned in narratives related to social change? What young leaders do you recall learning about? If you're like us, you can likely count the number on one hand (or perhaps, sadly, one finger). While young people's efforts are seldom prominently featured in the annals of history, young people have consistently played a pivotal role in advocating for and inspiring transformative social change (Gonzalez et al., 2024). Indeed, young people have a long history of fearlessly working to advance issues of equity and access, both in the United States and around the world (Braxton, 2016).

In 1899, a group of angry New York City newsboys went on strike to demand fair compensation for their work distributing the city's newspapers. Their actions inspired the largest child strike in US history, leading to improved employment terms for newsboys and shaping future child welfare laws (Bartoletti, 2003). The Civil Rights Movement in the United States serves as another compelling example of youth advocacy, where activists like John Lewis and Diane Nash were instrumental in fighting for racial equality (Wallace & Collier, 2023). As the chairman of the Student Nonviolent Coordinating Committee (SNCC) at age 23, John Lewis organized sit-ins and was one of the original Freedom Riders, challenging the segregation laws of the southern United States. Diane Nash, a leader within the same committee and also age 23, was instrumental in organizing the Freedom Rides and the Selma voting rights campaign, which were crucial in highlighting injustices and pushing for legislative change.

Similarly, in the anti-apartheid struggle in South Africa, young South Africans were at the forefront of resistance. In his twenties, Steve Biko, the founder of the Black Consciousness Movement, galvanized a large number of Black students and disenfranchised

individuals through a philosophy that emphasized pride and self-reliance, despite the oppressive apartheid regime (Soni, 2016). The activism of these young individuals not only involved protests but also played a strategic role in shaping public opinion and policy. This included the Soweto Uprising in 1976, where thousands of Black students protested against the mandatory use of Afrikaans in schools—a direct challenge to the apartheid system. These examples underscore the enduring impact of young people in challenging societal norms and driving movements that promote social justice, demonstrating their crucial role in both leadership and grassroots mobilization.

 Teaching Tip:

When spotlighting youth leaders in your classroom or youth-serving organization, focus on young people whose work is relevant to your discipline. For example, if you teach art or music, highlight the efforts of young people around the world who are advocating to advance art education in K-12 schools.

For more recent examples, consider the impact of young people in shaping social change discourse amidst the rise of social media activism, with marginalized groups, including people of color, LGBTQIA+ and disabled youth, turning to networking sites to advance counterstories by challenging mainstream perspectives (Jackson et al., 2020) on issues like sexual assault, racial discrimination, and climate justice. Examples include youth-led movements like the Arab Spring, where young activists used social media to contest oppressive regimes; Occupy Wall Street, critiquing economic inequalities; the #MeToo movement, amplifying stories of sexual harassment and assault; and the global climate strikes initiated by Greta Thunberg when she was 15 years old, advocating for urgent environmental action.

> **Activity Spotlight: Youth-Led Movements**
>
> Divide students into small groups and instruct them to research a youth-led movement or group and present the story of their findings through an artistic piece using their preferred medium. Debrief presentations with questions related to challenges and successes the young leaders experienced and what insights students gained from the activity. Below are some examples of youth-led movements and groups:
>
> - Student Nonviolent Coordinating Committee (SNCC)
> - Soweto Uprising
> - The Children's Crusade
> - Arab Spring
> - March for Our Lives
> - Pride vs. White County School District
> - Greensboro Sit-Ins
> - White Rose
> - School Walkouts Against Climate Change
> - Chilean Student Protests
> - Occupy Wall Street
> - Standing Rock

Below is an art piece, created by high school student Koi Hooker, depicting the story of the Children's Crusade to end segregation in Birmingham, Alabama. The piece illustrates children marching on the American flag, demonstrating how their efforts, which led to the Civil Rights Act of 1964, paved the way for a more equitable future.

Created by Koi Hooker

The text reads:

Children WILL pave the way for America

Research shows that youth participation helps movements succeed; young people expand movement coalitions by working across traditional societal lines, leveraging digital tools, rejecting party affiliations, and calling for systemic change (Cebul, 2023). Case in point: The 2019 youth-led Global Climate Strike, the culmination of 13 months of weekly school climate protests, propelled youth climate activism into the international media spotlight, mobilizing youth and adult allies from more than 185 countries around the world and drawing wide-reaching support from both policymakers and the scientific community (Hagedorn et al., 2019). Indeed, young people's commitment to social causes, particularly when paired with the skills and knowledge to convey an effective message, can shift public opinion and change behavior. For example, a study conducted by researchers at North Carolina State University found that young people can be instrumental in cultivating climate concern among their parents, especially when given the appropriate educational tools (Lawson et al., 2019).

> **Teaching Tip:**
>
> Most social change, whether small or large scale, starts locally. Encourage students to identify young people and youth-centered organizations in their communities working to address inequities in their schools and neighborhoods.

Amplifying Youth Voices Through Curriculum and Representation

As we learned from Bishop's mirror metaphor (1990) earlier in this chapter, representation matters. One of our book's guiding principles—*youth-led stories have and can drive social change*—speaks to the importance of amplifying young people's contributions. Yet despite their evident historical and contemporary contributions (Braxton, 2016), young people's efforts are all too often trivialized or outright dismissed by adults. Take the case of civil rights activist Claudette Colvin, whose refusal to give up her seat to a white woman on a segregated bus led to the 1955 Montgomery Bus Boycott. While her courageous actions preceded those of Rosa Parks, Colvin never received due credit for her efforts, largely because of her age (15), but also because she was pregnant and unmarried at the time (Adler, 2009).

> **Activity Spotlight: Youth Changemaker Trivia**
>
> Test students' knowledge of young leaders, past and present, who have left a meaningful imprint on their communities and the world. Students' responses, or lack thereof, can serve as an entry point to a broader dialogue about the need for greater youth representation in curricula. We've outlined a few sample trivia questions to get you started and encourage you to identify and add contemporary local examples to this list.
>
> - Before Rosa Parks, this 15-year-old student was arrested after refusing to give up her seat to a white woman on a segregated bus.
>   - *Answer: Claudette Colvin*

> - During Nazi Germany, this non-violent, student-led resistance group conducted an anonymous leaflet campaign that called for active opposition to the Nazi regime. As a result, many were charged with treason and sentenced to death.
>   - *Answer: The White Rose*
> - In this North Carolina city, four Black college students staged a sit-in at a local Woolworth, sparking sit-ins across the South and ultimately paving the way for desegregation in North Carolina.
>   - *The Greensboro Four*
> - At age 16, this environmental activist became the youngest person to be named *Time*'s Person of the Year for her role in mobilizing millions of people across 150 countries to protest for climate justice.
>   - *Greta Thunberg*

Given the lack of nuanced and accurate representation of youth leadership in the general curriculum, it's no wonder that youth often find themselves sidelined (Cebul, 2023), pigeonholed into a narrative that portrays them as either too "woke" and idealistic on the one hand or overly naive and inexperienced on the other (Gonzalez et al., 2024). The pervasiveness of such narratives can discourage youth leadership. In addition, the oversight of incorporating youth experiences and voices in the curriculum can cause an incomplete and skewed representation of historical, let alone social change, narratives. In contrast, positive and nuanced representation of youth leadership aids in countering the negative impact of youth-related stereotypes while building students' confidence in their capacity to contribute meaningfully to their schools and communities (Christens & Peterson, 2012; Gonzalez et al., 2024), which can be both validating and empowering.

> **Activity Spotlight: Curricular Analysis of Youth Representation**
>
> This reflective exercise is an opportunity for students to analyze and seek ways to increase youth representation in your classroom.
>
> - Divide participants into small groups.
> - Provide each group with large sheets of paper and markers.
> - Instruct groups to analyze books, lesson plans, and other curricular materials in terms of youth representation, focusing on the frequency with which young people are represented and how they are depicted.
> - Ask students to identify areas where the stories of young leaders could be incorporated, reframed, or expanded.
> - Discuss the potential impact of increased positive and nuanced youth representation.
>
> Drawing on student feedback, integrate youth perspectives into your curriculum by including readings, case studies, and discussions that highlight historical and contemporary contributions of young changemakers.

Fostering Positive and Productive Youth–Adult Partnerships

Beyond representation, centering students means thinking intentionally about how we can empower their efforts. Youth–adult partnerships, a concept popularized in youth development literature, emphasize intergenerational equity and meaningful student participation (Chong, 2006). When implemented effectively, youth–adult partnerships have been shown to increase student engagement, improve learning outcomes, and nurture connection and leadership (Kokozos & Gonzalez, 2024).

For instance, at Riverside High School, a group of neurodivergent students expressed frustration with the lack of understanding and support for their unique learning needs. Recognizing the need for change, the school counselor, Mr. Hernandez, partnered with a local neurodiversity advocacy organization to establish a Neurodiversity Alliance Club. This student-led club was not simply a space for socializing but a platform for advocacy and change. With guidance from Mr. Hernandez and the advocacy organization, the students researched neurodiversity, identified barriers to inclusion within the school, and developed a comprehensive proposal for creating a more neurodiverse-affirming learning environment. They presented their findings and recommendations to the school administration, advocating for changes such as flexible seating arrangements, sensory-friendly spaces, and differentiated instruction strategies.

Despite the many documented benefits of positive youth–adult partnerships, a recent report by the Center for Resilient & Inclusive Societies (Baker & Ali, 2022) revealed that young people are often frustrated by collaborative relationships with adults. Mapping social justice-related concerns among youth, participants highlighted several considerations adults should consider when working with youth. For instance, young people often face mental health challenges, such as anxiety and depression, as they engage in social justice efforts. They also experience difficulties forming meaningful relationships with adult allies and often find themselves in spaces where important conditions related to power and privilege are overlooked. For example, youth from low-income backgrounds may be lacking some of the basic resources, like transportation, needed to participate in extracurricular activities or leadership opportunities.

Within educational and community-based settings, adults often inadvertently impose structural constraints on youth, which can undermine the effectiveness of their contributions and hinder the partnership (Checkoway, 2011). In the case of the Neurodiversity Alliance Club, Mr. Hernandez initially found himself trying to control the direction of the club's activities.

However, he quickly realized that the students had a deep understanding of their own needs and could lead the charge for change. This issue extends into the political sphere, where hierarchical structures dominated by adults contribute to a growing sense of disillusionment among young individuals (Gordon, 2010). Such dynamics often result in tokenization, whereby youth are symbolically included in initiatives without real, meaningful engagement or decision-making opportunities. This tokenization is apparent during school disciplinary hearings where students may be present but have yet to be given a voice in decision-making.

Educators and youth-serving professionals must actively challenge these practices by fostering environments that genuinely value and integrate youth perspectives. These efforts involve including young people in discussions and empowering them to take lead roles in planning and decision-making. Instead of tokenistic representation, schools can create youth-led committees with decision-making authority on issues impacting them, such as curriculum development, disciplinary policies, or school-wide events. By doing so, we can help nurture a generation of students who feel genuinely involved and valued in their communities and beyond.

To effectively gauge and improve our efforts in engaging young people, we can utilize the "Ladder of Youth Voice" developed by Roger Hart (1992) and adapted by Adam Fletcher (see Figure 6.1). This graphic illustrates varying levels of youth participation, from non-participation to full citizenship, including stages like manipulation, decoration, tokenism, and youth-initiated shared decisions (Fletcher, 2011; Hart, 1994). In the context of our discussions on the marginalization of youth in various domains, the graphic also becomes a valuable tool for reflection: We all can evaluate the extent to which youth engagement in our spheres of influence is meaningful or tends to be superficial and tokenistic. It prompts a critical examination of the extent to which young people are valued and meaningfully involved in collaborative efforts and decision-making processes.

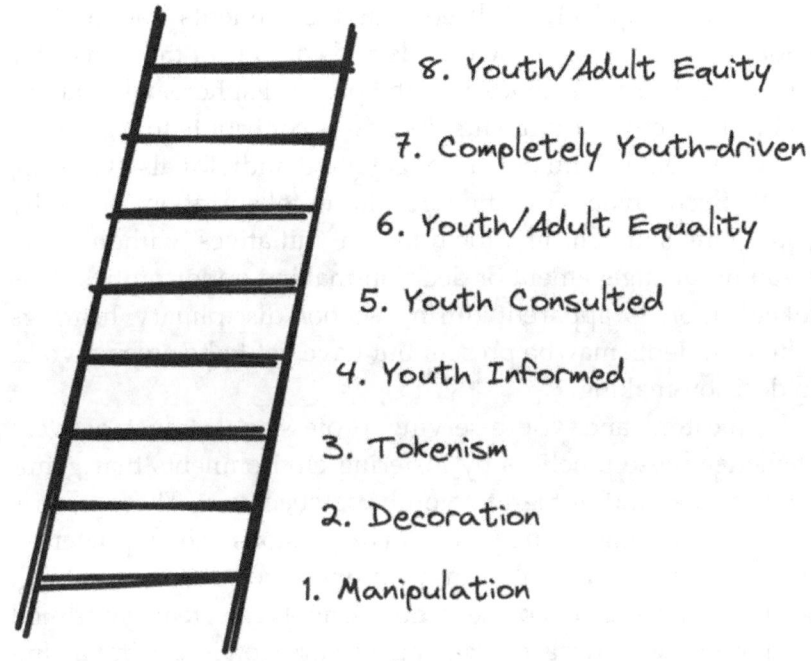

FIGURE 6.1 VISUALIZATION, THE LADDER OF YOUTH VOICE
Source: Adapted by Fletcher (2011) from work by Hart (1992)

 Activity Spotlight: Ladder of Youth Voice Reflection

Engage yourself or students in reflective exercises using the "Ladder of Youth Voice" to evaluate the extent of meaningful youth engagement in your classroom, school, or youth-serving organization. Discuss and analyze where their voices fall on the ladder and explore ways to move toward more meaningful involvement.

0. **Non-participation:** Youth have no role or voice in projects or decisions.
1. **Manipulation:** Adults use youth to support their own agendas without genuine youth input.
2. **Decoration:** Youth are included for appearances but have no real influence.

3. **Tokenism:** Youth are given limited opportunities for input and lack decision-making power.
4. **Youth Informed:** Youth are assigned roles and tasks and are informed about the project's goals and progress.
5. **Youth Consulted:** Adults actively seek youth input and opinions, but decisions ultimately rest with adults.
6. **Youth/Adult Equality:** Adults initiate projects and share decision-making power with youth.
7. **Completely Youth-Driven:** Youth initiate and lead projects, collaborating with adults as partners and mentors.
8. **Youth/Adult Equity:** Youth have complete ownership and control of projects, with adults providing support as needed.

In the case of the Neurodiversity Alliance Club, the initial stages of the project might have fallen under "Youth Informed" or "Youth Consulted," with Mr. Hernandez and the advocacy organization guiding the students' research and providing resources. However, as the students gained more confidence and expertise, they moved toward "Youth/Adult Equality" and eventually "Completely Youth-Driven," taking ownership of the project and advocating for change within their school. This progression demonstrates the importance of gradually increasing youth leadership and decision-making power as students develop their skills and knowledge.

Concluding Thoughts

Centering youth in social change narratives is not just a pedagogical approach; it's a commitment to fostering culturally sustaining and student-centered learning environments that spotlight historical and contemporary youth changemakers,

bridge gaps of representation, and foster authentic and genuine youth–adult partnerships. Such environments allow students to more clearly see the value of their own experiences and to believe more deeply in their capacity to build and share stories for social impact.

> **Questions for Extended Student Dialogue**
>
> - How and to what extent, if at all, did learning about youth leadership change your view about your capacity to drive social change?
> - What are the challenges facing young leaders? What benefits or opportunities do young leaders have when advocating for change?
> - What does your school or community organization do to support and encourage youth leadership in general and as it relates to social change specifically?
> - What else can your school or community organization do to support youth leadership?

> **Questions to Encourage Educator Self-Reflection**
>
> - Think back to your experience in middle or high school. What did your teachers do (or not do) to promote youth voice and leadership? What impact did their actions have on you?
> - What steps do you currently take to support and encourage youth leadership, in general and related to social change? What impact do these actions have on your students or the youth you work with?
> - The article recommends keeping an open mind, actively listening, and valuing students' perspectives,

> even if they differ from your own. Think of a time when a student or young person shifted your thinking about a social issue. What did you learn from that experience?
> ♦ How can you collaborate with students or young people in ways that center and amplify their voices?

References

Adler, M. (2009, March 15). Before Rosa Parks, there was Claudette Colvin. *National Public Radio*. www.npr.org/2009/03/15/101719889/before-rosa-parks-there-was-claudette-colvin

Arnold, M. E., & Gagnon, R. J. (2020). Positive youth development theory in practice: An update on the 4-H thriving model. *Journal of Youth Development*, 15(16), 1–23. https://doi.org/10.5195/jyd.2020.954

Baker, A., & Ali, L. (2022). *Mapping young people's social justice concerns: An exploration of voice and action*. Centre for Resilient and Inclusive Societies. (n.d.). www.crisconsortium.org/research-reports/young-people-social-justice

Ballard, P. J., & Ozer, E. (2016). The implications of youth activism for health and wellbeing. In J. O. Conner & S. M. Rosen (Eds.), *Contemporary youth activism: Advancing social justice in the United States* (pp. 223–244). Praeger.

Bartoletti, S. C. (2003). *Kids on strike!* Clarion Books.

Bishop, R. S. (1990). Mirrors, windows, sliding glass doors. *Perspectives: Choosing and Using Books for the Classroom*, 6(3), ix–xi.

Braxton, E. (2016). Youth leadership for social justice: Past and present. In J. Conner & S. Rosen (Eds.), *Contemporary youth activism: Advancing social justice in the United States* (pp. 25–38). Prager.

Cebul, M. (2023). *Youth activism: Balancing risk and reward*. United States Institute of Peace. www.usip.org/publications/2023/01/youth-activism-balancing-risk-and-reward

Checkoway, B. (2011). What is youth participation? *Children and Youth Services Review*, 33(2), 340–345.

Chong, J. (2006). Benefits of youth–adult partnerships. *Children and Family, 9*, 1–2. http://hdl.handle.net/10125/2763

Christens, B. D., & Peterson, A. N. (2012). The role of empowerment in youth development: A study of sociopolitical control as mediator of ecological systems' influence on developmental outcomes. *Journal of Youth and Adolescence, 41*, 623–645.

Fletcher, A. (2011). *Ladder of youth voice.* http://www.freechild.org/ladder.htm

Ginwright, S., & Cammarota, J. (2007). Youth activism in the urban community: Learning critical civic praxis within community organizations. *International Journal of Qualitative Studies in Education, 20*, 693–710. https://doi.org/10.1080/09518390701630833

Gonzalez, M., & Kokozos, M. (2019). Prejudice reduction in public schools: A dialogic approach. *Journal of Educational Research and Practice, 9*(1), 340–348. https://doi.org/10.5590/JERAP.2019.09.1.24

Gonzalez, M., Kokozos, M., Byrd, C., & McKee, K. (2020). Critical Positive Youth Development: A framework for centering critical consciousness. *Journal of Youth Development, 15*(6). https://doi.org/10.5195/jyd.2020.859

Gonzalez, M., Kokozos, M., McKee, K., & Byrd, C. (2024). Storytelling through a Critical Positive Youth Development framework: A mixed methods approach. *Journal of Youth Development, 19*(1). https://tigerprints.clemson.edu/jyd/vol19/iss1/2

Gordon, H. R. (2010). *We fight to win: Inequality and the politics of youth activism.* Rutgers University Press.

Hagedorn, G., Kalmus, P., Mann, M., Vicca, S., van den Berge, J., van Ypersele, J. P., ... & Hayhoe, K. (2019). Concerns of young protesters are justified. *Science, 364*(6436), 139–140. https://doi.org/10.1126/science.aax3807

Hart, R. (1992). *Children's participation: From tokenism to citizenship.* UNICEF, International Child Development Centre.

Jackson, S. J., Bailey, M., & Welles, B. F. (2020). *#Hashtagactivism: Networks of race and gender justice.* The MIT Press.

Kokozos, M., & Gonzalez, M. (2024). Collaboration & social change: Promising practices for effective youth-led partnerships. *Journal of Extension, 62*(3), 33.

Lawson, D. F., Stevenson, K. T., Peterson, M. N., Carrier, S. J., Strnad, R., & Seekamp, E. (2019). Children can foster climate change concern among their parents. *Nature Climate Change*, *9*, 458–462. https://doi.org/10.1038/s41558-019-0463-3

Lerner, R. M., Lerner, J. V., Almerigi, J., Theokas, C., Phelps, E., Gestsdóttir, S. Naudeau, S., Jelicic, H., Alberts, A. E., Ma, L., Smith, L. M., Bobek, D. L., Richman-Raphael, D., Simpson, I., Christiansen, E. D., & von Eye, A. (2005). Positive youth development, participation in community youth development programs, and community contributions of fifth-grade adolescents: Findings from the first wave of the 4-H Study of Positive Youth Development. *Journal of Early Adolescence*, *25*(1), 17–71.

Moll, L. C., Amanti, C., Neff, D., & Gonzalez, N. (1992). Funds of knowledge for teaching: Using a qualitative approach to connect homes and classrooms. *Theory into Practice*, *31*(2), 132–141.

Paris, D. (2012). Culturally sustaining pedagogy: A needed change in stance, terminology, and practice. *Educational Researcher*, *41*(3), 93–97.

Soni, M. (2016). *When lions roared: How brave young people defied apartheid*. NUMA.

Wallace, S. N., & Collier, B. (2023). *Love is loud: How Diane Nash led the Civil Rights Movement*. Simon & Schuster Books for Young Readers.

7

The Ethics of Storytelling

A group of middle schoolers buzz with excitement in the library. They're huddled around a laptop, brainstorming ideas for their upcoming project: a series of interviews with members of their community. They would like to explore the experiences of people facing homelessness.

"We could interview people at the shelter downtown," suggests Emily, the school's newspaper editor with a passion for social justice.

"Or maybe we could talk to the volunteers who run the food pantry," chimes in David, always eager to lend a helping hand.

Mr. Patel, their teacher, smiles at their enthusiasm. "These are great ideas," he says. "But before we start reaching out to people, let's talk about something important: how we tell these stories ethically."

A hush falls over the group. *Ethically?* they wonder. *What does that even mean?*

Ethical Considerations for Storytelling

Mr. Patel explains, "When we tell stories, especially stories about other people, we have a responsibility to be thoughtful and respectful. We need to ensure we're accurate and fair and protect the people we're interviewing." The students nod, intrigued, as they realize that storytelling isn't just about finding a good story but navigating

a complex web of ethical choices. As these middle schoolers embark on their project, they'll grapple with questions like:

- How do we build trust with the people we interview?
- How do we ensure we're representing their stories accurately and fairly?
- What are the potential implications of sharing these stories for the individuals involved and the wider community?

These are just a few considerations that storytellers must navigate. As emphasized in our guiding principles for teaching storytelling, *ethics are essential*. In the following sections, we'll delve deeper into these complexities, providing you with the tools and strategies to implement ethical storytelling practices.

So, what do we mean by ethics in the context of storytelling?

In the simplest terms, ethics in storytelling involve treating the people whose stories we tell—and the audiences who hear those stories—with fairness, honesty, and respect (Documentary Accountability Working Group, 2022). Think of it like this: Imagine you're in your classroom, listening to your students share their personal experiences. You wouldn't want to twist their words, make assumptions about their lives, or share their stories without their permission, right? The same principles apply when we tell stories outside the classroom, whether as journalists, filmmakers, or simply sharing anecdotes with friends.

For us, social impact storytelling ensures we are ethically minded by aligning with the following core values:

- **Respect:** Honoring the voices and experiences of those we represent.
- **Truthfulness:** Striving for accuracy and avoiding the spread of misinformation.
- **Empathy:** Approaching topics with curiosity, care, and understanding.
- **Accountability:** Taking responsibility for the impact of our narratives.
- **Allyship:** Using our storytelling power to amplify marginalized voices and challenge injustice.

Social impact storytelling isn't so much about following rules as it's about cultivating a mindset of responsibility and compassion; it's about recognizing the power of stories to shape our understanding of the world and using that power for good.

> **Activity Spotlight: Ethics Free Association**
>
> Work with students to examine the associations they have to the word "ethics" using the prompts below.
>
> - **Individual Reflection:** Think about the word "ethics." What words, phrases, or emotions immediately come to mind? Jot down your thoughts.
> - **Group Sharing:** Share your lists with a partner or small group. Notice any common themes or surprising connections within your group.
> - **Class Discussion:** As a class, discuss the following questions:
>   - What patterns or themes emerged from this free association exercise?
>   - How do these words and phrases relate to storytelling?
>   - Why might ethics be important in the context of storytelling?

Respect

Mr. Patel's class is passionate about exploring the issue of homelessness. While their initial idea of interviewing individuals directly is well-intentioned, it's important to consider the potential vulnerabilities of this population and the power dynamics at play. Instead of focusing solely on firsthand interviews, Mr. Patel suggests alternative approaches that still enable students to engage with the topic meaningfully and ethically.

To broaden their understanding, he prompts students to examine the historical and systemic factors contributing to homelessness, shifting the narrative away from individual experiences and toward understanding the broader social forces at play.

For example, they can analyze existing media coverage, documentaries, and scholarly articles to gain a better understanding of the complexities of the issue. Instead of directly interviewing individuals experiencing homelessness, students can seek out experts and advocates working in the field, like social workers, shelter staff, or representatives from organizations dedicated to addressing homelessness. These individuals can provide valuable insights and perspectives without potentially exposing vulnerable individuals (e.g., refugees, survivors of trauma) to further scrutiny or discomfort (Voice of Witness, n.d.).

> **Activity Spotlight: Guiding Students in Brainstorming Ethical Approaches to Storytelling**
>
> When exploring sensitive topics, facilitate a brainstorming session to generate ethically grounded and impactful storytelling approaches. Use these guiding questions to spark creative thinking and ensure meaningful engagement:
>
> - How can we learn about this issue without directly interviewing people who might be vulnerable?
> - How can we use different storytelling mediums (e.g., art, music, writing, etc.) to explore this topic?
> - What community resources or organizations can we collaborate with to gain insights and perspectives?
> - How can we create stories that raise awareness and inspire action without causing harm or perpetuating stereotypes?

Truthfulness

Truthfulness stands as the cornerstone of social impact storytelling. We must present facts and realities accurately, even when they challenge prevailing narratives or force us to confront uncomfortable truths. This commitment to truthfulness fosters trust with our audiences, empowers them to make informed decisions, and upholds the integrity of the stories we tell.

Mr. Patel, keenly aware of the challenges posed by the information age, prioritizes truthfulness in his classroom. He introduces his students to the CRAAP test—Currency, Relevance, Authority, Accuracy, and Purpose—a framework for evaluating sources (Blakeslee, 2004). One day, he presents two articles on homelessness, one from a reputable news outlet and another from a blog known for its sensationalist headlines. He guides his students through the CRAAP test, helping them recognize the blog's lack of credible sources and its biased language, compared to the balanced reporting of the news article. He also shows them how misleading statistics can be used to paint a distorted picture of reality. For instance, he might highlight a statistic claiming a dramatic increase in homelessness without providing context about population growth or changes in data collection methods.

To go beyond surface-level portrayals of homelessness, Mr. Patel encourages his students to read first-person narratives from individuals experiencing homelessness, exploring the diversity of their experiences and the complex web of factors that led to their situations. They also study the systemic issues that perpetuate homelessness, such as lack of affordable housing, mental health disparities, and gaps in social safety nets. Mr. Patel models transparency by sharing his journey of learning about homelessness. He openly discusses his initial assumptions, the biases he had to confront, and the ongoing process of deepening his understanding. He creates a safe space for students to acknowledge their perspectives, even if they are incomplete or evolving. He emphasizes the importance of being open to feedback and correction, recognizing that truthfulness is an ongoing pursuit, not a fixed destination.

Activity Spotlight: Case Study—Artificial Intelligence and Storytelling

The rise of artificial intelligence (AI) in storytelling has opened exciting possibilities for creativity and innovation. AI-powered tools can generate story ideas, create compelling characters, and even compose music and art.

However, this technology also raises ethical questions about authenticity, bias, and the potential for manipulation. For instance, deepfake technology can create highly realistic fabricated videos, with the potential to spread misinformation (Westerlund, 2019). Additionally, if AI algorithms are trained on biased data, they can perpetuate harmful stereotypes and reinforce existing inequalities (O'Neil, 2016).

Before we dive deeper, let's make sure we all understand what AI is. AI involves creating computer systems capable of performing tasks that typically require human intelligence, such as learning, problem-solving, and decision-making (Russell & Norvig, 2016). Ask the class:

- What are some examples of AI you already know?
- How do you think AI works (in simple terms)?

Establishing Classroom Norms for AI

Now, let's establish norms for how we'll use AI in the classroom, especially for storytelling, to ensure we use this technology responsibly and ethically.

- **Brainstorm:** What are the potential benefits and drawbacks of using AI in storytelling?
- **Discussion:** What ethical concerns arise when using AI for storytelling? (e.g., plagiarism, bias, the importance of human creativity)
- **Guidelines:** Now, let's create a set of guidelines for how we can use AI responsibly and ethically in our classroom. These might include: always citing AI assistance; critically evaluating AI-generated content for bias; using AI as a tool to enhance, not replace, human creativity.

Critical Media Literacy

Guiding students in developing critical media literacy skills is crucial in today's information-saturated world (Kellner & Share, 2005). Empower students to become discerning consumers and creators of information by teaching them how to evaluate sources. Introduce the CRAAP test as a practical tool for assessing credibility. Provide examples of both credible and non-credible sources and guide students in applying the CRAAP test to analyze them. Discuss the importance of considering the author's expertise, the publication's reputation, and the evidence presented to support claims.

Equally important is helping students identify bias in media. Explain the concept of bias and how it can subtly or overtly influence how information is presented. Have students analyze various media sources (e.g., news articles, social media posts, advertisements) to identify different types of bias, such as omission (leaving out information), selection (choosing specific information), placement (where information is put), and labeling (using loaded words). Encourage them to consider the author's perspective, the language used, and the overall tone of the piece when evaluating bias.

 Teaching Tip:

Consider partnering with your school librarian or media specialist to incorporate media literacy lessons into your curriculum. These lessons help students develop the critical thinking skills necessary to navigate the complex digital landscape and make informed choices about the information they consume and share.

Furthermore, it is crucial to teach students to distinguish between factual statements that can be verified and opinions that express personal beliefs or judgments. Provide clear examples of each and then introduce more nuanced examples that blend the two. Engage students in discussions about how opinions can be presented as facts and how to identify these instances.

Fostering a culture of inquiry in your classroom is also essential. Encourage students to question the information they encounter, even from seemingly reliable sources. Teach them to ask probing questions like: "Who created this information?" "What is their purpose?" "What evidence is provided?" and "Are there other perspectives to consider?" Emphasize the importance of seeking out diverse viewpoints on any given issue. Encourage students to consult various sources, including those that challenge their perspectives. Discuss how exposure to different views can broaden understanding and lead to more informed decision-making.

Remember, you can make learning interactive and engaging by integrating media literacy activities into your curriculum across different subjects and using real-world examples. Model critical thinking yourself when analyzing media and information, inspiring your students to follow suit. By fostering these critical media literacy skills, you're equipping your students with the tools they need to navigate the complexities of the digital age, make informed choices, and become responsible and engaged citizens (Kellner & Share, 2019).

 Activity Spotlight: Fact-Checking Challenge

Present your students with a news article or social media post related to a social issue they are exploring. Have them work in groups to assess the accuracy and credibility of the information presented. Use guiding questions like:

- Who created this information? What is their perspective or potential bias?
- What evidence is provided to support the claims made in the story?
- Can you find similar information from other reliable sources?
- Are there any inconsistencies or contradictions in the information presented?

> ♦ What ethical considerations might have been involved in creating and sharing this story?
> ♦ Did the story uphold the values of respect and truthfulness?

By striving for accuracy and transparency, we uphold the integrity of stories. We empower our audiences to make informed decisions based on reliable information, and we avoid perpetuating harmful stereotypes or misinformation. Remember, truthfulness is not just about getting the facts right; it's also about presenting a complete and nuanced picture of reality. As educators, we play a vital role in fostering a culture of truthfulness in our classrooms. By modeling ethical research practices, encouraging critical thinking, and empowering students to question the information they encounter, we help them become responsible and informed storytellers.

Empathy

Empathy is the heart of ethical storytelling, particularly when dealing with social change topics. It involves putting ourselves in the shoes of others, seeking to understand their experiences, emotions, and perspectives, even if they differ from our own. Mr. Patel understands that empathy is a skill that needs to be cultivated. Before his students embark on interviews outside the classroom, he decides to create a safe space within it for them to practice empathy and perspective-taking, rooted in the guiding principle that *space matters*.

Recognizing that some students might initially approach such a personal activity with hesitation or even lightheartedness, Mr. Patel takes proactive steps to ensure its success and foster genuine empathy. To establish clear expectations, he initiates a class discussion, brainstorming specific behaviors that demonstrate respect and active listening. Together, they create a shared list of expectations that everyone agrees to follow. During the activity, Mr. Patel models these behaviors himself, demonstrating

attentive listening through eye contact, nodding, and verbal cues. He also provides gentle reminders, such as "Let's make sure we're giving our full attention to the person who is sharing," to redirect any off-task behavior.

Next, Mr. Patel carefully selects the prompts for the paired interviews, ensuring they encourage reflection and vulnerability without being overly intrusive or triggering. He provides examples like "Share a time when you felt misunderstood" or "Describe a challenge you overcame that made you stronger." He also reminds students that they have the right to decline to answer any question or share details they are uncomfortable with.

As the students begin their interviews, Mr. Patel circulates the room, observing their interactions and offering gentle guidance when needed. He notices that the initial giggles and awkwardness gradually give way to genuine curiosity and compassion. Students ask thoughtful follow-up questions, nod in understanding, and offer words of encouragement. By the end of the activity, the room is filled with a sense of connection and shared humanity. Students are learning to see the world through the eyes of their classmates, gaining a deeper appreciation for the diversity of human experiences.

 Activity Spotlight: Empathy Mapping

Introduce your students to empathy mapping, a powerful tool for cultivating empathy and perspective-taking. This visual exercise helps students imagine themselves in another person's shoes, fostering a deeper understanding of their thoughts, feelings, and actions.

Example Prompt:

- ◆ "Imagine you are a new student at a school where you don't know anyone. It's your first day, and you're feeling nervous and a little bit lost."

Creating the Empathy Map:
Provide students with a template divided into sections:

- Thinking: What might the new student be thinking? *("I hope I can find my classes." "Will I make any friends?")*
- Feeling: What emotions might they be experiencing? *(Nervous, anxious, excited, hopeful)*
- Seeing: What might they be observing in their surroundings? *(Crowded hallways, unfamiliar faces, classroom decorations)*
- Hearing: What sounds or words might be impactful to them? *(Bells ringing, laughter, conversations in the hallway)*
- Saying and Doing: What might they be saying or doing? *(Asking for directions, trying to make eye contact with other students, sitting alone at lunch)*

Encourage students to fill in each section based on the prompt and their own inferences. Then, have them share their maps and discuss the insights they gained.

Once students have practiced empathy mapping, challenge them to apply this skill to their storytelling. How can they use empathy maps to develop more well-rounded characters, craft authentic dialogue, and create narratives that resonate with their audience?

Accountability

Accountability is the backbone of ethical storytelling. It's about recognizing that every story we tell has an impact—on individuals, communities, and society as a whole. As storytellers, students must take ownership of their narratives, acknowledge their potential consequences, and be prepared to address any harm that may arise. Mr. Patel's students have poured their hearts into their research, interviews, and creative expressions. But before they hit "publish" or share their work with the world, Mr. Patel gathers them for one final discussion: accountability.

"Remember," he says, "our stories have the power to shape perceptions and influence how people view the issue of homelessness. We need to be mindful of our messages and the potential impact our words and images might have." He encourages his students to reflect on questions such as:

- Are we representing the voices and experiences of those we interviewed accurately and fairly?
- Could our stories inadvertently perpetuate stereotypes or reinforce harmful narratives?
- How might different audiences, including those directly affected by homelessness, receive our work?

This conversation sparks thoughtful dialogue among students. They realize that their responsibility as storytellers extends beyond simply creating compelling narratives. It's about ensuring that their stories are truthful and respectful and contribute to a more compassionate and just society.

 Teaching Tip:

To prioritize accountability, incorporate peer review into the storytelling process. During peer review, students can ask questions about specific facts, representation of different viewpoints, and potential sensitivities in the story. Emphasize providing constructive feedback, highlighting positive aspects, and maintaining open-mindedness during the process. This approach fosters critical thinking, empathy, and a deeper appreciation for the power of storytelling.

 Activity Spotlight: Accountability Check-In

Before students share their stories, have them complete an "accountability check-in," which could be a simple worksheet or a group discussion in which they reflect on their

> storytelling choices and consider the potential impact of their work. Encourage them to identify any areas where they could improve or make adjustments to ensure their stories are responsible and impactful.
>
> By instilling a sense of accountability in your students, you are empowering them to become conscious and responsible storytellers. You are helping them understand that their words and actions have consequences and that they are responsible for using their voices for good. Remember, accountability is not about perfection but a willingness to learn, grow, and make amends when necessary. By fostering a culture of accountability in your classroom, you are creating a space where students can explore complex social issues with integrity and compassion.

Allyship

Allyship in storytelling is a multi-faceted commitment to amplifying marginalized voices, challenging injustice, and creating a more equitable world. It's not just about telling stories; it's about using our narratives as a tool for social change, always mindful of the power dynamics at play. In practice, this might mean stepping back and recognizing that sometimes the most powerful act of allyship is simply creating space for others to tell their stories. It's about resisting the urge to insert ourselves into narratives that are not ours to tell, even with the best intentions. As educators, we can model this for our students by actively seeking out and sharing stories created by marginalized communities themselves rather than appropriating their experiences for our own purposes.

Mr. Patel, for instance, introduces his students to documentaries and written works created by individuals experiencing homelessness. He facilitates discussions where students analyze these narratives, paying close attention to the unique perspectives and insights offered by those with lived experiences. By prioritizing these authentic voices, he allows his students to connect with the unique experiences and perspectives of individuals

facing homelessness, fostering empathy and challenging stereotypes, and paving a path toward allyship.

Ethical storytelling as an ally requires more than simply amplifying marginalized voices. It demands consistent self-reflection and a commitment to dismantling oppressive systems. Storytellers must critically examine their biases and privileges, understanding how these factors influence their narrative choices. True allyship centers the voices and agency of those whose stories are being told, prioritizing their perspectives and respecting their control over their own narratives. Ethical storytelling becomes a tool for social change by challenging dominant narratives, exposing systemic injustices, and advocating for equity. This requires a conscious effort to avoid perpetuating harmful stereotypes and instead use narrative power responsibly, fostering narratives that reflect the lived realities of marginalized communities.

> **Teaching Tip:**
>
> Even with the best intentions, we can make mistakes in how we tell stories. Language is powerful, and stories can unintentionally perpetuate biases or cause harm. When stories cause intentional or unintentional harm, it's our responsibility to address the impact and take steps to repair the damage. This practice relates directly to our first guiding principle of teaching storytelling: *space matters*. Restorative practices offer a framework for addressing harm by focusing on healing, accountability, and reconciliation (Zehr, 2015). These practices, often used in other fields like justice and education, can be applied to storytelling.
> Here's how:
>
> ♦ **Acknowledge harm:** Openly acknowledge the harm caused by the story. This includes acknowledging the impact on individuals directly affected and the potential broader impact on communities.

- **Apologize sincerely:** Offer a genuine apology to those hurt or offended. A sincere apology is specific, acknowledges the impact of the harm, and expresses remorse.
- **Make amends:** Take concrete steps to repair the harm, such as:
  - **Correcting misinformation:** If the story spread false information, take steps to correct it and share accurate information.
  - **Offering support:** Provide support to those affected by the story, including emotional support, resources, or advocacy.
  - **Changing practices:** Revise your approach to storytelling to prevent similar harm in the future like seeking diverse perspectives, being more mindful of language choices, or reestablishing ethical guidelines.
- **Learn and grow:** Reflect on the experience and use it as an opportunity for growth.
- **Examine biases:** Consider your biases and assumptions that may have contributed to the harm.
- **Seek feedback:** Ask for feedback from others to understand the impact of your storytelling and identify areas for improvement.
- **Commit to change:** Make a commitment to do better in the future and use your storytelling for good.

Concluding Thoughts

As educators, we have a unique opportunity—and responsibility—to guide our students in developing their ethical storytelling skills. By fostering critical thinking, empathy, and cultural competence, we empower them to become not just storytellers, but *ethical* storytellers. This means teaching them to question assumptions, challenge dominant narratives, amplify

marginalized voices, and hold themselves accountable for the impact of their words and actions. However, the ethical imperative of storytelling extends far beyond the classroom. As consumers and creators of information, we are all called to engage with stories more mindfully and responsibly. In a world saturated with stories, it's easy to become complacent, accepting stories at face value without questioning their origins, biases, or potential consequences. By embracing ethical storytelling principles, we can transform narratives from mere entertainment into powerful tools for social change. We can use stories to bridge divides, challenge injustice, and amplify the voices of those who have been silenced. We can create a more informed, empathetic, and equitable society, one story at a time.

Questions for Extended Student Dialogue

- How can we balance the need for impactful stories with the responsibility to avoid sensationalism or exploitation?
- What are some strategies for incorporating diverse perspectives and avoiding stereotypes in storytelling?
- How can storytelling foster empathy, understanding, and connection between different communities?
- What role does critical media literacy play in ensuring ethical storytelling in the digital age?
- How can we hold ourselves and others accountable for the ethical implications of the stories we tell?

Questions to Encourage Educator Self-Reflection

- Am I creating a safe, inclusive space for students to share their stories and perspectives?
- Am I modeling ethical storytelling practices in my teaching?

- How can I support students in developing their critical thinking and media literacy skills to become more discerning consumers and creators of information?
- What steps can I take to promote diversity and inclusion in the stories and examples I share with students?
- Am I staying informed about the latest ethical debates and challenges in storytelling?

References

Blakeslee, S. (2004). The CRAAP test. *LOEX Quarterly, 31*(3). https://commons.emich.edu/loexquarterly/vol31/iss3/4

Documentary Accountability Working Group. (2022). *From reflection to release: Framework for values, ethics, and accountability in nonfiction filmmaking (VEA)*. www.docaccountability.org/framework

Kellner, D., & Share, J. (2005). Toward critical media literacy: Core concepts, debates, organizations, and policy. *Discourse: Studies in the Cultural Politics of Education, 26*(3), 369–386.

Kellner, D., & Share, J. (2019). *The critical media literacy guide: Engaging media and transforming education*. Brill Sense.

O'Neil, C. (2016). *Weapons of math destruction: How big data increases inequality and threatens democracy*. Crown.

Russell, S. J., & Norvig, P. (2016). *Artificial intelligence: A modern approach*. Pearson Education.

Voice of Witness. (n.d.). *VOW's ethical storytelling principles*. https://voiceofwitness.org/resource-library/ethical-storytelling-principles

Westerlund, M. (2019). The emergence of deepfake technology: A review. *Technology Innovation Management Review, 9*(11), 39–52.

Zehr, H. (2015). *The little book of restorative justice*. Good Books.

8

The Story of Me

Nurturing Personal Storytelling

The energy in Ms. Garcia's 10th-grade English class was palpable. A hush fell over the room as Jamal, usually the quietest student, began to speak. "The worn leather of my grandfather's baseball glove tells stories of games won and lost," he began, his voice soft but steady. "He taught me how to catch a fly ball, but more importantly, how to never give up." Jamal paused, a glimmer of pride in his eyes, "That glove is a part of me, a connection to my family and our history."

This simple three-sentence story exercise helped Jamal gain confidence as a storyteller; it also ignited a spark of curiosity and empathy in his classmates, who were eager to share their own experiences. This is the power of personal storytelling: it allows us to connect with ourselves and others, build understanding, and create a community of shared experiences (Gottschall, 2012).

In this chapter, we'll explore the power of personal storytelling within the classroom. We'll begin with low-stakes activities, such as crafting three-sentence stories, and gradually progress to more intricate storytelling forms, including testimonials and public narratives. Through these activities, we'll uncover how personal storytelling can nurture critical reflection, ultimately

empowering students to act as informed agents of change in their lives and communities.

 Activity Spotlight: The Three-Sentence Story

To dip our toes into personal storytelling, let's begin with a simple, low-stakes activity, like the one Jamal did in Ms. Garcia's class: the three-sentence story. This exercise is a chance to share a glimpse of your life, a memory, an observation, or even a random thought. It doesn't have to be serious or profound; it can be about anything that holds meaning for you. Keep it short and sweet, just three sentences to pique curiosity.

Here are a few additional examples to inspire your students:

- "The old oak tree in my backyard is my sanctuary. Its gnarled branches remind me of every climb. When I climb it, I feel connected to my ancestors and the land."
- "The first time I performed on stage, my knees shook like earthquakes. But when the spotlight hit, a wave of joy washed over me. I discovered a voice I never knew I had."
- "The aroma of freshly baked bread fills my grandmother's kitchen. I can still hear the laughter. I can still hear the clatter of pots and pans."

 Teaching Tip:

Try it now. Write a three-sentence story you can share with your students. Modeling these low-stakes tasks can create a safe space for others to share their stories.

Foundations of Personal Storytelling

The three-sentence stories we shared offer a glimpse into the power of personal stories, even in their most condensed form. For example, Jamal's story about his grandfather's baseball glove resonates because it captures the essence of a treasured relationship and family legacy. But what makes stories like Jamal's so compelling? How can we develop these snippets into richer, more meaningful stories?

Let's revisit the essential building blocks of storytelling—those fundamental elements that give narratives their shape and structure—which we first introduced in Chapter 1. As Clark and Rossiter (2006) suggest, understanding these elements not only deepens students' appreciation for the craft of storytelling but also empowers them to create more compelling and meaningful narratives. This understanding aligns with our guiding principle that *story structure matters*. To reinforce this, Ms. Garcia encourages her students to identify these building blocks in their stories and those shared by their classmates:

- *Setting:* The where and when of the story. It's the backdrop against which the events unfold.
- *Characters:* The individuals who populate the story and drive its action.
- *Conflict:* The challenge or problem that the characters face.
- *Resolution:* How the conflict is resolved or addressed.
- *Message:* The underlying theme or idea that the story conveys.

Understanding these elements is like having a roadmap for crafting personal stories. Imagine Jamal takes his three-sentence story and expands upon it. He introduces the setting: the sun-drenched Little League field where he practiced and the bleachers where he and his grandfather watched baseball games together. Then, he fleshes out the characters: the quirky

grandfather and his uncles who never failed to cheer Jamal on from the sidelines. He explores the conflict: how he struggled to live up to his grandfather's expectations and how the loss of the glove represented a deeper loss in their relationship. The resolution and message emerge from this conflict, revealing lessons learned about perseverance, family bonds, and the bittersweet nature of change.

Building on These Basics: Layering Narrative Complexity

Once students grasped the foundational elements, Ms. Garcia introduced a series of storytelling exercises to expand their narrative skills. The goal was to guide students beyond the initial three-sentence stories and encourage them to explore different narrative possibilities, incorporating more complex elements to create richer, more meaningful stories.

One exercise focused on developing compelling characters. Ms. Garcia asked students to choose a character from their life—a family member, friend, or even a stranger they observed—and write a detailed description of them. Students were encouraged to explore the character's personality, motivations, and quirks beyond physical appearances. This exercise helped students to develop their ability to create believable and engaging characters, a crucial aspect of any good story. For example, one student described a friend who, despite being incredibly shy, had a knack for making others laugh with his perfectly timed, self-deprecating jokes. Another described their grandmother whose quirky personality inspired countless stories—from her love of bright, mismatched clothing to leaving Post-It notes all over the house.

Another exercise explored the concept of conflict, the driving force behind many narratives. Students were asked to brainstorm a list of potential conflicts that could arise in their lives or the lives of their characters. They then selected one conflict and wrote a scene depicting the characters grappling with this challenge. This exercise helped students understand how conflict creates tension and drives a story forward.

As students experimented with these exercises, Ms. Garcia introduced additional narrative elements:

- *Plot:* Students learned how to structure their stories to keep the reader engaged, using rising action, climax, and falling action to create a satisfying arc.
- *Theme:* Ms. Garcia encouraged students to reflect on the deeper meaning of their stories, exploring the universal themes that connect us all, such as love, loss, identity, belonging, and the search for meaning.
- *Tone:* Students experimented with different tones, from humorous to somber, to create the desired mood and atmosphere.
- *Point of View:* They explored the different perspectives from which a story can be told, recognizing how the narrator's voice shapes the reader's experience.

A Student Example: Maya's Expanded Narrative

In Ms. Garcia's class, a student named Maya took up the challenge to expand her three-sentence story about the smell of pan de muerto in her grandmother's kitchen during Día de Muertos. She began by setting the scene: the warmth of the kitchen, the sweet scent of orange blossom and cinnamon filling the air, the colorful papel picado hanging from the ceiling. Maya's abuela, her hands stained with the vibrant hues of food coloring, meticulously crafted sugar skulls, each a tiny masterpiece representing a departed loved one.

> The marigolds blazed like tiny suns, their scent a mix of earth and sweetness. Abuela's voice, soft and steady, wove stories around me like the papel picado dancing in the breeze. She spoke of our ancestors, their laughter echoing through time, their strength coursing through our veins. I traced the delicate sugar skulls, each one a whisper of a life lived.

A lump formed in my throat as the candles flickered, casting long shadows. It wasn't sadness, not exactly. It was more like... a deep ache, knowing that even the most vibrant lives eventually fade. But Abuela's stories reminded me that they don't truly disappear. They live on in us, in the love we share, the traditions we carry. And as we raised our glasses of champurrado, toasting to those we missed, I felt a warmth spread through me, chasing away the shadows. It was the warmth of being part of something bigger than myself. And at that moment, I understood. Día de Muertos wasn't about mourning death; it was about celebrating life.

As you can see, Maya captures the essence of Día de Muertos through vivid sensory details and heartfelt emotions. The theme emerges as a celebration of life and remembrance, acknowledging the bittersweetness of honoring loved ones who have passed. From Maya's first-person perspective, the story paints a poignant picture of the holiday, highlighting the importance of storytelling in preserving cultural heritage and connecting with ancestors. Through her grandmother's tales and her own reflections, Maya deepens her understanding of the enduring power of memory, ultimately finding solace and strength.

Social impact storytelling, at its heart, is deeply personal. Keehn's (2015) research, for example, suggests that incorporating personal stories into the classroom can enhance student learning and engagement by creating a more relatable and emotionally resonant learning experience. And beginning with such personal moments, we have found, helps students to engage with their everyday experiences, emotions, and observations that shape their lives. Ms. Garcia recognized this, encouraging her students to first delve into their flashbulb memories as a starting point for self-expression. Through this personal exploration, she believed, students could begin to see how their

lives intersect with larger social and political forces. And once examined critically, these individual stories can illuminate, if not direct, students toward how we are all shaped by systems and structures that warrant scrutiny in the pursuit of social change.

Introducing Criticality: Unmasking Power Dynamics

With this foundation of personal storytelling in place, Ms. Garcia then guided her students toward a deeper level of analysis by introducing the concept of **criticality**. "Our stories are not just about us," she explained. "They are shaped by the world around us, by the systems and structures that influence our lives. When we tell stories, we can share our experiences and examine the forces that shape those experiences." She emphasized that developing a critical lens means questioning assumptions, analyzing information, and considering different perspectives. "It's about looking beyond the obvious," Ms. Garcia explained, "and digging deeper to understand the complexities of a situation."

For example, a student might write a story about feeling frustrated and unheard in their new school. While the newness and unfamiliarity of the environment are obvious factors, Ms. Garcia pushes them to go further. She wants them to consider if the school's structure itself contributes to their feelings. Are there limited opportunities for student voice and input? Do certain policies disproportionately affect some students? Is there a lack of diverse representation among teachers and staff? In essence, criticality encourages the students to challenge assumptions, analyze information, and consider different perspectives. They learn to identify the complex interplay of factors that shape their experiences and develop the skills necessary to analyze and interpret information in a more meaningful way.

Building on this foundation, Ms. Garcia introduced the concept of **critical reflection**, one of our guiding principles and a core component of the CPYD framework that grounds this book. Critical reflection is the awareness of social, political, and economic forces that shape our lives and the world around us. It involves understanding these forces and recognizing our agency and potential to challenge and change them. Ms. Garcia encouraged her students to use their stories to develop this awareness and to see how their personal experiences are connected to larger systems of power and inequality. A core component of critical reflection is understanding **power**, power dynamics, and our **positionality** within those dynamics.

To help her students grasp these complex concepts, Ms. Garcia drew upon the detailed exploration of power dynamics found in Chapter 5, introducing the different forms of power with clear examples. "Think about how the principal sets the rules in our school," she explains. "That's an example of institutional power—the power of organizations or systems to influence us." She went on to illustrate economic power with examples like the influence of wealthy individuals and the gap between rich and poor neighborhoods. To explain cultural power, she discussed how media shapes beauty standards and how social pressures enforce gender norms.

Ms. Garcia emphasized that grasping these power dynamics goes beyond simply identifying who holds power; it requires recognizing how power operates and the diverse ways we can analyze it. "Just like we use different lenses to see things more clearly," she explained, "we can use different 'lenses of power' to examine social issues." These lenses, outlined in the table below, allow students to focus on various aspects of power—whether institutional, economic, cultural, or even individual—and how they intersect and influence one another. By consciously choosing their lens, students can gain a more nuanced perspective on the forces at play, enabling them to critically analyze situations and challenge assumptions.

Lenses of Analysis

Lens of Analysis	Definition	Example
Individual	Focuses on the unique characteristics, experiences, and perspectives of a single person, including both internal and external factors.	A student reflects on how their upbringing in a rural community shaped their appreciation for nature and influenced their decision to pursue environmental studies.
Intrapersonal	Focuses on internal processes and dynamics within an individual.	A student recognizes how their anxiety about public speaking affects their ability to participate in class discussions.
Interpersonal	Examines interactions and relationships between individuals, including communication patterns, power dynamics, and conflict resolution.	A group of students collaborates on a project, learning to negotiate roles, share ideas, and resolve disagreements.
Cultural	Explores shared values, beliefs, and practices of a group, including how culture shapes identity, behavior, and social norms.	Students analyze how different cultural perspectives are represented in a novel, examining how these perspectives influence the characters' actions and interactions.
Institutional	Examines social structures, institutions, and systems, including how they influence individual and group behavior, create inequalities, and shape social change.	Students research the history of their schools, investigating how policies and practices have evolved over time and how they have impacted different groups of students.

She then posed thought-provoking questions to spark student engagement and encourage them to connect these abstract concepts to their own lives:

- "Can you think of an example where you've seen institutional power at play in your school or community?"
- "How might economic power affect someone's access to opportunities or resources?"
- "In what ways does cultural power shape our beliefs about what is 'normal' or 'acceptable'?"

Bridging to Personal Experience

To further solidify understanding, Ms. Garcia shared real-world examples that resonated with her students:

- She highlighted how school dress codes often disproportionately target girls and students of color, illustrating the intersection of institutional and cultural power.
- She discussed the challenges students from low-income families face in accessing educational resources, revealing the impact of economic power.
- She shared stories of individuals who challenged societal norms, demonstrating the potential for resisting cultural power.

 Teaching Tip:

Cultivating our critical reflection allows us to understand the world around us better and create more equitable and inclusive learning environments for our students (Palmer, 1998). To spark your own reflection, consider how you can apply the concept of positionality to your teaching practice. Reflect on how your social identities (e.g., race, class, gender, etc.) shape your perspectives and interactions with students. Consider how your positionality might influence your teaching style, curriculum choices, or classroom management strategies.

Exploring Positionality

To help students grasp the concept of positionality, Ms. Garcia explained that it refers to our social location—our race, class, gender, sexuality, and other aspects of our identity—and how this shapes our perspectives and experiences. "It's important to understand how our positionality influences how we see the world and the stories we tell," Ms. Garcia emphasized. "It can help us to recognize our own biases and assumptions and to be more open to the perspectives of others."

Privilege

Ms. Garcia recognized that fostering critical reflection also involves understanding the concept of privilege—the unearned advantages and benefits that certain individuals or groups receive based on their social identities (McIntosh, 1989). She facilitated a discussion about privilege, emphasizing that it doesn't negate individual struggles but rather highlights systemic inequalities. For instance, a student from a wealthy family might face personal challenges, but their socioeconomic status still affords them advantages that a student from a low-income background might not have. She encouraged students to reflect on their own privileges—perhaps being able-bodied, cisgender, or speaking the dominant language—and consider how these might contrast with the experiences of others. This exploration of privilege helped students develop a deeper understanding of power dynamics and their positionality within those dynamics (Freire, 1970).

 Activity Spotlight: Crafting a Testimonial

With a foundation of understanding power and privilege, Ms. Garcia introduced the testimonial activity as a tool for students to delve deeper into their personal narratives and explore the connections between their individual experiences and broader social issues. She began

by explaining the purpose and structure of a testimonial, emphasizing its potential for both self-expression and social analysis (Bernal et al., 2016). She then offered guiding prompts to help students reflect on and articulate their experiences:

Prompts for crafting a testimonial:

- **Describe the event or experience in detail.** What happened? Where were you? Who was involved? What were you feeling and thinking?
- **Analyze the power dynamics.** Who held power in the situation? How was that power expressed? Were there any imbalances of power or privilege?
- **Examine your positionality.** How did your race, class, gender, sexuality, or other aspects of your identity shape your experience? Did you feel empowered or disempowered? Privileged or marginalized?
- **Connect your experience to larger social issues.** How does your story reflect broader patterns of discrimination or inequality? What are the historical and systemic roots of these issues?
- **Call to action.** What can be done to address these issues? What practical solutions can we implement to create sustainable change?

 Teaching Tip:

Address false equivalencies. Facilitate discussions about the distinction between feeling uncomfortable in a new or unfamiliar situation and experiencing systemic oppression. Encourage students to be mindful of their privilege and to listen to the voices of those who have been historically marginalized.

Example:

> ♦ **Scenario:** A student expresses discomfort about being asked to consider their gender privilege during a discussion on feminism. They claim, "I've felt excluded before for being a man. Isn't that the same as sexism against women?"
> ♦ **Educator response (incorporating the tip):** "It's understandable to feel uneasy when exploring new concepts or challenging your own perspectives. That discomfort can be a sign of growth and learning. However, it's important to differentiate between personal experiences of exclusion and the systemic oppression faced by women throughout history and even today. While feeling left out in a specific situation is valid, it doesn't equate to the pervasive discrimination, limited opportunities, and violence that women experience due to their gender."

Remember, we all hold various privileges based on our identities. Being mindful of our privilege allows us to empathize with and better understand the experiences of those who face systemic oppression. It's crucial that we listen to and believe the voices of marginalized groups, even when it challenges our perspectives. And by carefully guiding students through this process, Ms. Garcia empowers her students to not only understand the complexities of power and privilege but also to use their voices and stories to advocate for themselves.

Here is an example from a Muslim student sharing a poignant story with the class:

When I wear a hijab, I often feel like I'm under a microscope. People stare, whisper, and sometimes even make rude comments. One day, on a field trip to the city, I was separated from my classmates during a security check at a museum. The guard pulled me aside and searched my bag

while everyone else watched. I felt singled out because of my headscarf. At that moment, I felt the weight of all the stereotypes and prejudices that people hold about Muslims. I was no longer just Aisha, a student on a field trip; I was a symbol of fear and suspicion. My experience is not unique. Many Muslims, especially women who wear the hijab, face similar situations. This prejudice isn't just about a single incident; it's about systemic discrimination rooted in Islamophobia. I want to use my voice to challenge these harmful stereotypes and build bridges of understanding between different cultures. We need to educate ourselves and others about Islam, celebrate diversity, and reject prejudice in all its forms.

> **Teaching Tip:**
>
> Pause and reflect. How does Aisha's story make you feel? What does it reveal about the power of personal narratives in challenging stereotypes and promoting social justice? How does your positionality shape your understanding of Aisha's experience? In what ways might you use your positionality to contribute to a more inclusive and equitable world?

Bridging Personal to Public: The Power of Shared Narratives

Aisha's testimonial underscores the connection between personal experiences and the broader public narratives that shape society (Ganz, 2009). Her story of facing prejudice while wearing a hijab resonates with countless others who have encountered discrimination based on their religious or cultural identity. It's a stark reminder that individual experiences are often reflections of systemic inequalities (Bell, 2003, 2009).

Imagine a student named Alex growing up in a small town with limited access to arts education. Alex has always been passionate about painting but feels constrained by the lack of

opportunities in their community. They dream of attending a prestigious art school but worry about the financial burden it would place on their family. Similarly, Alex's story of limited access to arts education highlights a broader narrative about educational inequity and the barriers faced by students from underserved communities. Their dreams and frustrations resonate with others navigating similar challenges, underscoring the power of individual stories to illuminate systemic issues.

The "Story of Self" and Public Narrative

These individual stories, while powerful on their own, gain even greater significance when connected to broader public narratives. A "Story of Self" is not just a personal anecdote; it's a way to share the values that define who we are and how those values connect to the world around us. By reflecting on our experiences and the choices we've made, we can uncover the "moral sources" (Taylor, 1989) that motivate us to engage in social change.

Crafting a "Story of Self" allows us to bridge the personal and the public, demonstrating how our individual experiences are intertwined with larger social issues and inspiring others to join us in the pursuit of justice and equity. This process involves identifying key "choice points" in our lives—moments when we faced challenges, made decisions, and learned valuable lessons that shaped our values and beliefs (Hammack, 2008). By sharing these stories authentically, we can build credibility and connection with audiences, inviting them to understand our motivations and join us in the work of advancing equity.

Guiding Questions for Crafting a "Story of Self"

- What are the key "choice points" in your life that have shaped your values and beliefs?
- When did you first become aware of the social issue you care about?
- What experiences have motivated you to take action?

- What challenges have you faced, and how have you overcome them?
- What lessons have you learned, and how do those lessons inform your advocacy?

> **Activity Spotlight: "Story of Me" Collage—Connecting Personal to Public**
>
> - Have students create a collage visually representing their personal story and its connection to a broader social issue.
> - They can convey their message through images, words, symbols, or other creative elements.
> - Encourage them to share their collages with the class and explain the connections they've made.
>
> As Lambert (2013) notes, incorporating multimedia elements into storytelling can further enhance engagement and allow students to express themselves in diverse ways.

Story Circles

While crafting a "Story of Self" is a powerful individual exercise, sharing those stories in a collective setting can amplify their impact and foster a deeper sense of community and shared purpose. This is where Story Circles come in. Story Circles contribute to collective sharing, creating a space where individual voices come together to further learn and connect with one another. In this format, participants sit in a circle and take turns sharing stories, focusing on active listening and respectful feedback.

Story Circles have roots in many Indigenous traditions around the world and have been adapted for use in various settings, including schools, community organizations, and therapy groups (Deardorff, 2020). They provide a space for participants to share their experiences, listen to each other's stories, and learn from one another; in addition, they can help build empathy, challenge

stereotypes, and find common ground (see Deardorff, 2020 for a comprehensive guide). This practice, however, requires skilled facilitation. While often well-intentioned, Story Circles can inadvertently perpetuate the very systems of oppression they seek to dismantle. Consider these scenarios:

- A workplace story circle where a manager's presence, however supportive, subtly discourages open dialogue about workplace harassment.
- A community gathering where one voice dominates, leaving marginalized perspectives unheard and unexpressed.
- A sharing circle focused on personal challenges, lacking clear guidelines for emotional safety, potentially retraumatizing participants.
- A seemingly diverse group where a lack of cultural understanding leads to appropriation rather than appreciation.

These scenarios are reminders that even the most seemingly benign practices can carry the weight of unexamined power and privilege. If the Story Circle's shadows loom too large, alternatives exist, including:

- *Journaling*, which provides a private space for students to explore their thoughts, feelings, and experiences, and connect those experiences to broader social issues. We encourage students to use journals as a tool for self-discovery, critical thinking, and personal growth.
- *Structured discussion groups*, which offer a more focused and guided approach to dialogue. By providing clear guidelines, prompts, and protocols, educators can create a safe and productive space for students to share their perspectives, listen to others, and engage in thoughtful conversations around specific themes.
- *Peer mentoring* creates opportunities for students to connect with each other on a more personal level, offering support, guidance, and encouragement. By pairing

students with peers who have shared experiences or interests, educators can foster a sense of belonging and create a supportive network for learning and growth.

If the Story Circle still calls to you, review Chapter 2 on creating trust, community, and connection. In that spirit and complemented by the conceptual and analytical work of Ms. Garcia's class, here are some guidelines to mitigate harm and maximize the potential for Story Circles:

- ♦ Explicitly state that hateful or discriminatory views will not be tolerated.
  - Begin the Story Circle by establishing clear ground rules.
  - State explicitly that any language or behavior that is hateful, discriminatory, or disrespectful toward any individual or group will not be tolerated.
  - Provide examples of unacceptable behavior, such as personal attacks, stereotypes, and hate speech.
- ♦ Acknowledge power dynamics and actively work to decentralize them.
  - Be mindful of the power dynamics that may exist within the group, such as those based on age, gender, race, or social status.
  - Encourage participants to share their stories and perspectives equally, ensuring that no one voice dominates the conversation.
  - Use a talking piece to ensure that everyone has an equal opportunity to speak without interruption.
  - If a participant with more power (e.g., a teacher in a classroom setting) is sharing, encourage them to be mindful of their position and create space for others to share their experiences.
- ♦ Establish clear agreements prioritizing emotional safety, confidentiality, and active listening.
  - Co-create a set of agreements with the participants that prioritize emotional safety, such as respecting

each other's feelings, avoiding judgment, and using "I" statements when sharing personal experiences.
- Emphasize the importance of confidentiality, ensuring that what is shared in the circle stays in the circle.
- Encourage active listening by reminding participants to pay attention, avoid interrupting, and ask clarifying questions.

◆ Center marginalized voices and create space for their experiences to be heard and validated.
- Be mindful of who is speaking and whose stories are being centered.
- If certain voices are dominating the conversation, gently redirect the focus to create space for those who haven't had a chance to share.
- Use prompts or questions that specifically encourage marginalized voices to share their experiences.
- Acknowledge and validate the experiences of marginalized individuals, even if they are difficult or challenging to hear.

◆ Link storytelling to action, providing concrete opportunities for participants to address systemic issues and create positive change.
- After sharing stories, facilitate a discussion about the common themes and issues that emerged.
- Brainstorm potential actions that participants can take to address those issues, either individually or collectively.
- Provide resources and support for participants to engage in advocacy or community organizing efforts.
- Encourage participants to share their stories with a wider audience to raise awareness and inspire change.

No matter which path you choose, focus on critical reflection. Reflect on your intentions, examine your privilege, and commit to creating spaces that are truly safe, inclusive, and empowering for

all. The journey toward social justice and emotional well-being is not linear. Here are a few examples of prompts that can be used:

- ♦ "Share a story about a time when you felt unseen or unheard."
- ♦ "Tell us about a moment when you realized the power of your voice."
- ♦ "Describe a time when you challenged a stereotype or assumption about your identity."
- ♦ "Share a story about a person or event that inspired you to take action for social justice."

Concluding Thoughts

Personal storytelling is an ongoing process of self-discovery, connection, and empowerment. By creating spaces where students feel safe to share their stories, educators can nurture critical reflection, empathy, and a sense of agency. Remember that storytelling is not just about the individual; it's also about how those individual narratives connect to broader social issues and inspire collective action.

Moreover, we will build upon this foundation in the subsequent chapters, exploring the "story of us" and the "story of now." We'll explore how collective narratives shape communities and examine the present moment and its implications for the future. By understanding these additional components of public narratives, we can empower students to become active participants in shaping their environments and inspiring others to do the same.

But first, we will explore the dynamics of dominant and counterstories. Aisha's experience sheds light on the pervasive influence of dominant narratives—those powerful stories that shape our perceptions and perpetuate systems of oppression. The next chapter will explore how these dominant narratives operate and how counterstories, like Aisha's testimonial, can challenge and reshape them. We will examine the role of power in shaping

narratives and discuss strategies for using storytelling as a tool for social justice and liberation.

Questions for Extended Student Dialogue

- How has sharing your personal story impacted your understanding of yourself and your location in the world?
- In what ways did writing your testimonial help you connect your personal experience to a larger social issue?
- What are some ways you can incorporate storytelling into your life, both personally and academically?
- Reflecting on the concept of positionality, how do your unique background and experiences influence the stories you tell and how you interpret the stories of others?
- How can storytelling bridge cultural divides and promote understanding between different communities?

Questions to Encourage Educator Self-Reflection

- How can I create a safe and supportive environment for students to share their stories?
- How can I integrate storytelling into my curriculum in a meaningful and engaging way?
- How can I use storytelling to promote critical thinking and social justice in my classroom?
- What are some ways I can continue to develop my storytelling skills and practices?
- How can I use storytelling to build stronger relationships with my students and foster community in the classroom?

References

Bell, L. A. (2003). Telling tales: What stories can teach us about racism. *Race, Ethnicity and Education*, *6*(1), 3–28.

Bell, L. A. (2009). The story of the storytelling project: An arts-based race and social justice curriculum. *Storytelling, Self, Society*, *5*, 107–118.

Bernal, D. D., Burciaga, R., & Carmona, J. F. (2012) Chicana/Latina testimonios: Mapping the methodological, pedagogical, and political. *Equity & Excellence in Education*, *45*(3), 363–372. doi:10.1080/10665684.2012.698149

Clark, M. C., & Rossiter, M. (2006). "Now the pieces are in place...": Learning through personal storytelling in the adult classroom. *New Horizons in Adult Education and Human Resource Development*, *20*(3), 19–33.

Deardorff, D. K. (2020). *Manual for developing intercultural competencies: Story Circles*. UNESCO.

Freire, P. (1970). *Pedagogy of the oppressed*. Continuum.

Ganz, M. (2009). *What is public narrative: Self, us & now* (Public Narrative Worksheet). Working Paper.

Gottschall, J. (2012). *The storytelling animal: How stories make us human*. Houghton Mifflin Harcourt.

Hammack, P. L. (2008). Narrative and the cultural psychology of identity. *Personality and Social Psychology Review*, *12*(3), 222–247.

Keehn, M. G. (2015). "When you tell a personal story, I kind of perk up a little bit more": An examination of student learning from listening to personal stories in two social diversity courses. *Equity & Excellence in Education*, *48*, 373–391.

Lambert, J. (2013). *Digital storytelling: Capturing lives, creating community*. Routledge.

McIntosh, P. (1989). White privilege: Unpacking the invisible knapsack. *Peace and Freedom Magazine*, *10*(1), 10–12.

Palmer, P. J. (1998). *The courage to teach: Exploring the inner landscape of a teacher's life*. Jossey-Bass.

Taylor, C. (1989). *Sources of the self: The making of the modern identity*. Harvard University Press.

9

Exploring Dominant Narratives and Counterstories

On Anna's first day as the 4-H Youth Development Agent in Pine County, she almost turned the car around and drove back to her apartment three times. The thought of all those yet-to-be-unpacked boxes in her lonely apartment kept her on course. She felt sick with nerves, wondering whether or not she would be able to connect with Pine County kids—their lives were so different from hers! And she had heard *stories* from the previous agent and some of her professors about how tough kids from this part of the state could be and how limited the resources were to support them. How could she build a teen council that was active in county and state programs if the kids were disinterested and couldn't afford program fees? How could she build a network of volunteers in a place where people surely didn't have time to volunteer?

In a panic, she called a mentor who had worked in a similar community and asked for help. Her mentor reminded Anna that the stories you hear and read shape how you think about events, yourselves, who you can be, and who other people can be. For every human experience, there is a prevailing story that sets the idea of what is normal or possible. These dominant narratives are a quiet but powerful force in shaping what you believe about your roles, your families, your communities, and more. Anna's predecessor and professors had shared the dominant narratives

about low income communities and communities of color with her and this limited who she thought her 4-H youth and families could be.

> **Dominant narrative:** An account of events that reflects the position of people in power to further their interests and ideologies.
> **Counterstory:** An account of events told from the perspective of someone who has been historically marginalized, oppressed, excluded, or silenced.
> **Implicit Bias:** Attitudes or stereotypes that impact understanding, behavior, and decisions in our interactions with others.

Identifying Dominant Narratives

A dominant narrative reflects the perspectives and ideas of people who are in power—that is, people who have the ability to decide what stories get told. The stories we see in popular culture are a reflection of the people who get to decide what books, movies, songs, and TV shows get made. The stories in our textbooks and class readings are a reflection of the people who write curricula and the boards that approve them. This means that the stories we hear most frequently—the dominant narratives—are decided upon by the people who have the power to access roles that control the stories such as producers and studio heads, publishers, and school board members.

Dominant narratives promote the interests and ideas of the dominant social group with the intention of making these interests and ideas—such as who can be a doctor or president, who excels in schools, what a family looks like, who should participate in a sport or activity, how historical events unfolded, or who we should see in movies—seem normal and natural and all others seem strange or against nature (Johnson et al., 2017). For example, US History textbooks tell the story of the Alamo from the American perspective only. It is taught as a symbol

of Texas's resistance to Mexico and was a rallying cry for the Texas Revolution that eventually led to the Mexican state of Tejas becoming a self-governing republic, Texas. The story told in Mexico is different. It includes that Tejanos fought on both sides of the conflict and were not unified against Mexican rule. Additionally, the story told in Mexico emphasizes the strength of Santa Ana's military leadership in securing a decisive victory. The dominant narrative is bound to a context and shaped by the people who control the storytelling in that context.

It is essential that we identify these dominant narratives and reflect on how they have impacted our ideas about people and the ways we engage with them. Anna spent the rest of her drive that first day, and many days thereafter, reflecting on where each idea she had about the people of Pine County had come from. She worked to connect the stories she had heard to the powerful ideologies that shaped them so that she could uncover her implicit biases, as these biases would interfere with her ability to connect to the community and work with the people in it. As she parked her car, she remembered all of the times someone had misconceptions about who she was and how that had limited her work with them. She decided that she wanted the 4-H youth and families to shape how she saw them instead of outsiders' opinions.

 Teaching Tip:

Most students are used to hearing or reading dominant narratives and some of them benefit from these narratives or believe that they do. A student whose life closely resembles the dominant narrative may not recognize the ways that their options and experiences have been limited or shaped by it and thus may only see that they benefit from being what they are "supposed to be." Further, they may be upset by the realization that they have been privileged by stories that made their path and choices seem natural and thus removed barriers to success that other students may

experience. Because of this, they may resist critical examination of the stories as attacks on them. Likewise, many students in your classroom or community organization may be harmed by dominant narratives. Dominant narratives can cause harm to students who are traditionally left out such as students of color, LGBTQIA+ students, or students who identify as women in fields dominated by men. The emotional response these stories provoke can create safety needs that can interfere with their participation in class. To mitigate both responses, we suggest starting with historical or fictional dominant narrative examples to practice identifying and critically examining dominant narratives.

 Activity Spotlight: Unpacking Dominant Narratives and Counterstories

Break students into groups of two to three and provide each group with a brief example of a dominant narrative such as: the American Dream; being good at school means you are smart; if you work hard, you will succeed; and youth are naive and idealistic.

1. Have each student read the example and discuss with their group: What is the overarching message? What does the person telling this story want you to believe? Where have you heard this story before?
2. Have each group develop an answer to: Who do you hear saying things like this? Why would they say it? Who benefits from this story? What is the purpose of telling this story? How is this story attempting to influence my thinking?
3. Have each group share their answers with the class. As a class discuss: Where do these stories come

from? Who benefits from them? Who would tell a different story? Who is silenced in this text?
4. What are the essential elements of the stories you read? (are taught as the absolute truth, are repeated frequently and without critique, benefit the people in power, ignore other perspectives)
5. Present the students with the definitions of dominant narratives and counterstories outlined in this chapter.
6. Ask whether the examples you provided were dominant narratives or counterstories. Then ask who could write a counterstory.

The Importance of Counterstories

Recognizing and challenging dominant narratives is crucial, but it's equally important to amplify the voices and experiences that those narratives often silence. This is where counterstories come in. For example, until very recently, the dominant narrative of women's gymnastics at the Olympic level was that the gymnasts were white women who typically competed for one or two Olympic cycles. When Dominique Dawes qualified for the US Women's Gymnastics Team for the 1992 Olympic Games, she was the first Black woman to do so. Her story was a counterstory. She then competed in the 1996 and 2000 games furthering her story as a counterstory as only two women had ever competed for the US in three games previously. When Gabby Douglas made the 2012 team, and went on to win the All-Around gold medal, her story was still a counterstory. Simone Biles credits seeing Gabby compete and become an Olympic champion with showing her it was possible and motivating her to train harder and work toward the Olympics.

In addition to helping people see possibilities left out of the dominant narrative, counterstories can influence the dominant narrative as more people become aware of these stories and the lives they represent over time. The dominant narrative may incorporate new elements taken from counterstories or the

counterstories can become new co-dominant narratives as they rise in public awareness. While Dominique and Gabby's stories were counterstories, the dominant story has started to change. Simone Biles' position on the team and as the All-Around gold medalist in 2016, Sunisa Lee's gold medal and Rebeca Andrade's (Brazil) silver medal wins in 2020, and Simone's gold medal repeat with Rachel Andrade winning silver and Sunisa Lee winning bronze in the 2024 games have all changed the story about who Olympic gymnastics is for, who can be a champion, and how long someone can stay at the top of the sport.

Anna spent some time researching counterstories and learned that personal stories told from the perspectives we don't often hear inspire social change by raising consciousness and helping us all learn. They contradict the deficit lens that is often applied to stories about communities of color and other marginalized people (Milner & Howard, 2013). Their inclusion disrupts the traditional representation of events and people (Demoiny & Ferraras-Stone, 2018) and can create settings where educators and youth can discuss oppression, marginalization, and critical action openly and work toward new understandings of topics such as racism and cultural exclusion (Ender, 2019).

Anna sought out autobiographical and composite counterstories in published works (Solórzano & Yosso, 2002) such as Maya Angelou's *I Know Why the Caged Bird Sings*, the *March* and *Run* graphic novels about John Lewis by Lewis, Andrew Aydin, and Nate Powell, and Turner's (2022) *Counterstories of High School Black Males' Experiences of the Mainstream Curricula*. And she listened to the stories people in the community told her about themselves and their youth. It is essential that counterstories come from the perspectives and voices of the people experiencing and working to counter oppression, in order to support their agency and tell truthful stories (Mora, 2014). Thus, in teaching students to read and develop counterstories, educators must provide them with strategies to determine the authenticity of the stories they read and to develop stories that are true to their own experiences. As Anna was still new to the community and didn't know the reality of the lives of the youth and adult volunteers she worked with, she decided to ask them to show her through a community walk.

> **Teaching Tip:**
>
> Organize a student-led community walk for the educators in your program. Ask students to develop an itinerary and path and explain important components of the community. This tour can serve as a counterstory that teaches the educators—and students—about their students and community. If a walking tour is not practical or accessible, have students record and present tours of their community to you. As you engage in these tours, ask yourself the questions included for educator self-reflection at the end of this chapter.

Ethical counterstories. As detailed in Chapter 7 and reflected in our guiding principles, we have a responsibility to ensure that our stories are accurate and respectful. Ethical storytelling requires a commitment to truthfulness, respectfulness, empowerment, and transformation. In order for a counterstory to support the empowerment and agency of the people in it, the story must be written and told from their perspective and with attention to truthfulness (Mora, 2014). Many books, movies, and shows have fallen short of this by trying to tell someone else's story without a deep understanding of their perspectives and reality. The result of this is the furthering of stereotypes and tokenisms that fail to represent real people's lived experiences. A recent example is the 2018 novel *American Dirt* by Jeanine Cummins, which purports to tell the story of a Mexican woman and her son who emigrated to the US to flee a drug cartel. The author, who is neither Mexican nor an immigrant to the US, defended the story saying "I did the work, I did five years of research" (Weiner & Advani, 2020); however, critics of the book who are immigrants from Mexico said that it does not reflect their experience, that they've never come across an immigrant whose experience is reflected in the novel, that it fetishizes trauma, and that they found harmful stereotypes in the book—"all these things that constantly make us feel small" (Grady, 2020; Gurba, 2019; Weiner & Advani, 2020). The author claims that these are industry issues and not her problem to fix (Weiner & Advani, 2020).

A storyteller must constantly assess the stories they are writing against the core ethical principles discussed in Chapter 7: respect, truthfulness, empathy, accountability, and allyship. One way to connect students with the importance of this ethical code is to have them work on telling their own stories the way they want them told. As you begin the process of developing counterstories with your students, review these guidelines in Chapter 7 to ensure that they have considered the implications of the stories they will tell and whether they are the best people to tell those stories.

> **Activity Spotlight: Identifying and Analyzing Counterstories**
>
> Develop a class list of stories that serve as counterstories, for example, The *March* and *Run* graphic novels by John Lewis (for grades 8 and up) or the *Mother Country Radicals* podcast by Zayd Dohrn.
>
> 1. Develop groups of two to three students and have each group choose one of the counterstories from the list.
> 2. Have each group research the subject of the counterstory and the author to answer: What is the author's connection to the story? Who benefits from the story? Who is empowered? What stereotypes are confronted or supported?
> 3. Have each group share with the class at least three key points as to why the author is, or is not, the appropriate person to tell the story.
> 4. As a class, develop guidelines for who you believe can tell someone's story.

Developing Autobiographical Counterstories

Asking the students in your classroom or program to write autobiographical counterstories—counterstories about themselves and from their experiences—can resolve the question of who is

the best person to tell their stories. Doing so can help students develop deeper understandings of their realities (Ender, 2019) as they work to deconstruct their personal experiences, the biases they hold, and their worldviews (Love, 2004) through this experience. As these experiences, biases, and worldviews are often unexplored, the work of developing their own story can empower youth, build clarity about their experiences, and expose others to stories that are currently missing (Ender, 2021).

You can begin by encouraging students to examine the dominant narratives critically as outlined in the first activity in this chapter. In every interaction you have with students, you can scaffold the skills and community building necessary to engage in critical examination of one's self and relation to the dominant narrative. This can be accomplished through clear community expectations as discussed in Chapter 2 and structured program time for short icebreakers to explore identity, intentional examination of personal connections to the course content, and sharing of writing in small groups for feedback (Song, 2019).

 Activity Spotlight: Lyrical Analysis

Spike Lee asked Public Enemy to write an anthem for his 1989 movie *Do the Right Thing*—a story of racial tension in a big city. The year before, Bobby McFerrin's *Don't Worry, Be Happy* had spent two weeks at the top of the Billboard charts and won three Grammy Awards. It offers a dominant narrative about letting go of the things that hurt you and choosing to be happy instead. Public Enemy's *Fight the Power*—written for Lee's movie—calls this out as a narrative that inhibits working for change as people who don't worry won't protest or engage in movements.

1. Have students listen to *Don't Worry, Be Happy* first and provide them with the lyrics.
2. Working in pairs or small groups, students should underline or highlight the lyrics that best summarize the message of the song.

3. Share with the whole group.
4. Have students listen to *Fight the Power* and provide them with the lyrics. You may need to use the radio edit version as the original contains language that some parents would object to their youth hearing. Please screen the version you use ahead of class time to be sure.
5. Working in pairs or small groups, students should underline or highlight the lyrics that best summarize the message of the song.
6. Share with the whole group.
7. As a class, work to answer, "How is *Fight the Power* a counterstory to *Don't Worry, Be Happy?*"

With this as an example of counterstories in song, return to your list of common dominant narratives and have each student select one to which they can write an autobiographical counterstory that they would be comfortable sharing. It is important to let the students choose so that they can tell stories they are comfortable sharing.

Throughout this text, we have shared multiple formats for storytelling; they would all be appropriate for developing an autobiographical counterstory. Additionally, Kokozos and Gonzalez (2021) provide a guide to resources to support counterstorytelling which provide samples of formats students might use. However, we suggest using the Blackout poetry format first. For additional information about blackout poetry, including a student example and facilitation guidelines, see Chapter 3.

1. Once each student has chosen a dominant narrative to address with their counterstory, have them find an example of a short story, poem, or song lyric that expresses the dominant narrative.
2. Tell students to consider this story from their perspective. Have them draw a line through any portions that do not resonate as true for them. Note

that it is possible, or even likely, that they will strike out the entire thing.
3. Share the created poems within small groups and ask each other: Which words did you choose to keep? In what ways do they resonate with you?
4. Debrief as a class: What did you notice about our poems? What similarities did you see? What differences? What surprised you? What does this say about the way all of us are seen or represented in these dominant narratives?

Next, provide the students with a template for an "I am from" poem.

1. Ask them to work individually to develop a poem using the template and the same counterstory theme they used in the blackout poem.
2. Have students share within their small group and discuss how they chose words to use.
3. Ask for volunteers to share with the class.
4. Debrief with: How was this experience different from writing the blackout poems? Which is a better representation of you? Why?

Extend the activity by allowing students to choose an additional format to tell their story.

1. Ask them to work individually to develop their counterstory in a format of their choosing.
2. Have students share within their small group and discuss how they built their story.
3. Ask for volunteers to share with the class.
4. Debrief with: How was this experience different from writing the blackout poems? And how was it different from writing the "I am from" poem? Which is a better representation of you? Why?

Recognizing Implicit Biases

In order for sharing stories to be an empowering and positive experience for students, you must prepare yourself to honor them as sources of knowledge and people with agency (Song, 2019). While you would never intend to fetishize or patronize their identities (Song, 2019), your implicit biases will be communicated as you work together (Byrnes et al., 1997; Vezzali et al., 2012); thus, you must engage in intentional work on your implicit biases (Byrnes et al., 1997; Vezzali et al., 2012). Tools such as the Implicit Association Test (Project Implicit, 2011) can uncover some of your biases (Grays et al., 2023), and practical empathy interventions can decrease implicit bias (Whitford & Emerson, 2019). Practical empathy interventions such as active listening, perspective taking, validating other's emotions, and mindfulness practice can help us develop and refine the ability to understand someone else's feelings and perspectives and respond with sensitivity.

For Anna, the student-led community walks helped build her understanding of the communities youth come from, the identities embodied therein, and the assets of the community that drive the stories youth build about themselves (Bateman & McCausland, 2020). However, she understood that it is essential to engage in critical self-reflection whenever she recognizes a thought or action that interferes with her ability to maintain openness to learning and engagement (Song, 2019). Questions for self-reflection are included at the end of this chapter.

Concluding Thoughts

Developing, sharing, and hearing counterstories can help students examine their life stories and learn more about themselves and each other. Further, these stories can help us better understand students' lives and communities. The process of telling one's story, especially when it is not the story we typically

hear, is empowering for youth if they can choose what to share and how to share it and are doing so in a supportive space. This requires us, as educators, to set and enforce community standards for listening and respect while continuously addressing our own biases and perceptions. If we are unsure whether students are ready to hear each other's stories and be supportive, we can begin with counterstories from other sources, such as those identified by Kokozus and Gonzalez (2021), which we have linked in the references.

Next, we'll continue to build on what we've learned in this and other chapters by outlining additional practices for helping students build effective social impact stories.

Questions for Extended Student Dialogue

- Why does telling your story matter to you?
- Think about a time when you heard a story about an event that was different from your story of it.
  - How did you react?
  - How would you react in the future knowing what you know now?
- What makes you comfortable to share your counterstory?
- What have you learned about yourself or your identity through writing an autobiographical counterstory?

Questions to Encourage Facilitator Self-Reflection

- In what ways do the dominant narratives in your field/subject reflect your identity?
- How has your identity framed the ways in which you teach your field/subject?
- How have you worked to learn about the diverse backgrounds your students embody?

- ♦ As far as you know, in what ways do the dominant narratives in your field/subject reflect your students' identities?
- ♦ When you share counterstories in class, how do you ensure that you are not perpetuating harmful stereotypes and tropes?

This chapter was written by Dr. Katherine McKee, Associate Professor at North Carolina State University.

References

Angelou, M. (1969). *I know why the caged bird sings*. Random House.

Bateman, K., & McCausland, J. (2020). Partnerships for culturally relevant and sustaining pedagogies through community walks and mapping. In M. Gresalfi & I. S. Horn (Eds.), *The Interdisciplinarity of the Learning Sciences, 14th International Conference of the Learning Sciences (ICLS) 2020*, Volume 4 (pp. 2371–2372). International Society of the Learning Sciences. https://repository.isls.org//handle/1/6565

Byrnes, D., Kiger, G., & Manning, M. L. (1997). Teachers' attitudes about language diversity. *Teaching and Teacher Education*, *13*(6), 637–644. http://doi.org/10.1016/S0742-051X(97)80006-6

Demoiny, S. B., & Ferraras-Stone, J. (2018). Critical literacy in elementary social studies: Juxtaposing historical master and counter narratives in picture books. *The Social Studies*, *109*(2), 64–73.

Ender, T. (2019). Counter-narratives as resistance: Creating critical social studies spaces with communities. *Journal of Social Studies Research*, *43*(2), 133–143. https://doi.org/10.1016/j.jssr.2018.11.002

Ender, T. (2021). Using counter-narratives to expand from the margins. *Curriculum Inquiry*, *51*(4), 437–454. https://doi-org.prox.lib.ncsu.edu/10.1080/03626784.2021.1947733

Grady, C. (2020). The controversy over the new immigration novel American Dirt, explained. *Vox*. www.vox.com/culture/2020/1/22/21075629/american-dirt-controversy-explained-jeanine-cummins-oprah-flatiron

Grays, A., Moise, D., Moore, E., Young, F., & Wilder, T. (2023). Why are we whispering? Addressing implicit bias in K-12 education. *SRATE Journal*, *32*(1).

Gurba, M. (2019, December). Pendeja, you ain't Steinbeck: My Bronca with fake-ass social justice literature. *Tropics of Meta*. https://tropicsofmeta.com/2019/12/12/pendeja-you-aint-steinbeck-my-bronca-with-fake-ass-social-justice-literature/

Johnson, L. L., Gibbs Grey, T. D., & Baker-Bell, A. (2017). Changing the dominant narrative: A call for using storytelling as language and literacy theory, research methodology, and practice. *Journal of Literacy Research*, *49*(4), 467–475. https://doi.org/10.1177/1086296X17733492

Kokozus, M., & Gonzalez, M. (2021). Cultivating critical consciousness in the classroom: 10 counternarrative resources. *Getting Smart*. www.gettingsmart.com/2021/02/15/cultivating-critical-consciousness-in-the-classroom-ten-counternarrative-resources/

Lewis, J., & Aydin, A. (2021). *Run*. Penguin Random House.

Lewis, J., Aydin, A., & Powell, N. (2013). *March: Book one*. Penguin Random House.

Lewis, J., Aydin, A., & Powell, N. (2015). *March: Book two*. Penguin Random House.

Lewis, J., Aydin, A., & Powell, N. (2016). *March: Book three*. Penguin Random House.

Love, B. J. (2004). Brown plus 50 counter-storytelling: A critical race theory analysis of the "majoritarian achievement gap" story. *Equity & Excellence in Education*, *37*(3), 227–246.

Milner, H. R., IV, & Howard, T. C. (2013). Counter-narrative as method: Race, policy, and research for teacher education. *Race Ethnicity and Education*, *16*(4), 536–561.

Mora, R. A. (2014). *Counter-narrative*. https://centerforinterculturaldialogue.files.wordpress.com/2014/10/key-concept-counter-narrative.pdf

Project Implicit. (2011). *Implicit association test (IAT)*. Harvard University. https://implicit.harvard.edu/implicit/takeatest.html

Solórzano, D. G. & Yosso, T. J. (2002). Critical race methodology: Counter-storytelling as an analytical framework for educational research. *Qualitative Inquiry*, *8*(1), 23–44.

Song, A-Y. (2019). Voice and experience: Forming counter-narratives through personal poetry. *EnglishJournal*, *108*(3), 74–80.

Turner, K. (2022). *Counterstories of high school Black males and their experiences of the mainstream curricula* (Publication no. 2360) [Doctoral dissertation, Georgia Southern University]. https://digitalcommons.georgiasouthern.edu/etd/2360

Vezzali, L., Giovannini, D., & Capozza, D. (2012). Social antecedents of children's implicit prejudice: Direct contact, extended contact, explicit and implicit teachers' prejudice. *European Journal of Developmental Psychology*, *9*(5), 569–581. http://doi.org/10.1080/17405629.2011.631298

Weiner, L., & Advani, R. E. P. (Producers). (2020). Latinx critics speak out against "American Dirt"; Jeanine Cummins responds. *Morning Edition*. NPR. www.npr.org/2020/01/24/798894249/latinx-critics-speak-out-against-american-dirt-jeanine-cummins-responds

Whitford, D. K., & Emerson, A. M. (2019). Empathy intervention to reduce implicit bias in pre-service teachers. *Psychological Reports*, *122*(2). https://doi.org/10.1177/00332941187674

10

Idea to Impact

Additional Practices for Effective Storytelling

When it comes to storytelling, generating an idea is half the battle. Brainstorming and reflection are key to building a story that is well-informed, thoughtfully executed, ethically grounded, and meaningful. Below are some additional activities and tips to jumpstart the storybuilding process and help students move from idea to impact.

Make a List

Making lists in response to a prompt helps combat writer's block by putting ideas on paper and laying the foundation for story creation. Here are some of our favorite list-making prompts for developing social impact stories:

- ♦ List reasons people should care about your topic.
- ♦ Make a list of actions that can or should be taken to make change around your topic.

- Who are the people and organizations with whom you can collaborate to motivate change and create awareness about your topic?
- List the ways you are connected to your topic.
- What would your school, community, and/or world look like if your vision of change was realized?

Develop a Story Structure

After students have had ample time to brainstorm ideas, encourage them to develop a narrative arc for their story, clearly delineating the beginning, middle, and end, though not necessarily in that order. Students whose stories place less emphasis on narrative (e.g., visual arts, videos, and photography) should still be encouraged to jot down their ideas and reflections and solicit feedback. Additional information related to story structure can be found in Chapter 1.

Encourage Reflection

Reflection is a key part of the story creation process. To increase impact, students should be reflective of how their stories are being shaped. That is, what sources are informing their main points? How are their social identities, biases, and lived experiences guiding how they tell their stories and what points they choose to emphasize? Reflection also affords students the opportunity to consider how and the extent to which they are establishing trust with and appealing to the audience's emotions and sense of logic. Students must also be mindful of their audience and tailor their message accordingly. For example, policymakers will likely be more interested in data, statistics, and the nuances of policy than a lay audience.

The following list of guiding questions for effective and ethical storytelling—developed by us, the authors of this book (Gonzalez et al., 2023)—is a reflective tool meant to encourage

student reflection before, during, and after the story creation and delivery process.

- What is the primary focus of your story?
- What do you hope to accomplish by sharing your story?
- What medium will you use to tell your story and how does the medium you are using shape the intended impact of your story?
- How are your identities and lived experiences shaping the focus of your story and how you choose to tell it?
- How are you establishing legitimacy as the storyteller?
- How might your story connect with people emotionally?
- Is your story informed by credible sources?
- Is there anything in your story that could be interpreted as offensive or divisive?
- If you are integrating a secondhand account(s) into your story, what are you doing to ensure your interpretation of the subject's experience is accurately represented?
- With whom might you collaborate to expand the scope of your message?

Use Organizational Tools

Graphic organizers and concept maps are effective ways to help students organize their thoughts and ideas. The Message Box, designed by COMPASS and printed below with permission (see Figure 10.1), is especially useful for providing structure to stories that are meant for public consumption. Students should begin in the middle of the box by identifying the overarching goal of their story and their intended audience. Starting here will help build

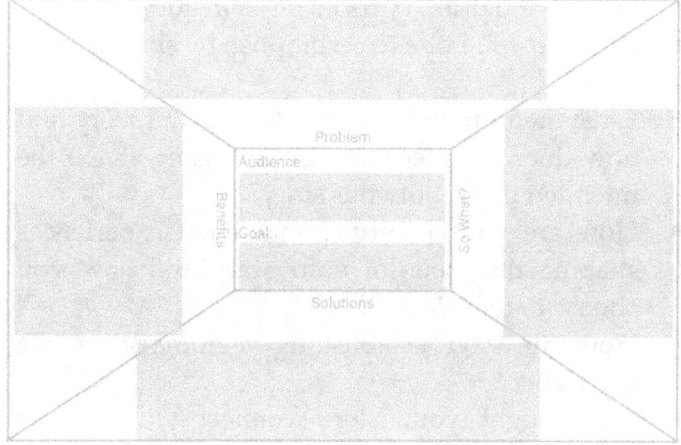

FIGURE 10.1 THE COMPASS MESSAGE BOX.
COMPASS is a non-profit organization that provides workshops and tools for strategic communication to improve the well-being of people and nature. Learn more about their work at www.compassscicomm.org
Source: COMPASS Science Communication (2023)

a communication strategy, shaping how key points and ideas are communicated.

The outer part of the Message Box consists of four boxes, which have been explained in greater detail below. For each box, students should aim to write one to two short sentences, focusing on the most important points and ensuring their message is consistent and aligns with their goal. Encourage students to include one or two brief examples in each of the four outer boxes to help reiterate their message. Examples of completed Message Boxes are available on the COMPASS website. Prior to completing the four outer boxes, students should identify their target audience and reflect on the overarching goal of their story (i.e., What do they hope the audience takes away from their message? What potential action might they hope to inspire?).

♦ Problem: What is the issue the student is seeking to address?

- So what? Why should your audience care about this issue? How does it impact them?
- Solutions: What steps can the audience take, individually and collectively, to address the issue?
- Benefits: In what ways will your audience benefit if the issue is successfully addressed?

 Teaching Tip:

Because storybuilding is an iterative process, peer review and feedback are essential. Encourage students to engage in peer review throughout the story creation process, including sharing their message boxes. Using prompts, like the ones provided below, will help ensure feedback is specific, kind, and constructive.

- Is the focus of the story clear?
- What specific aspect(s) of the story are particularly strong?
- What aspects of the story require further elaboration?
- What points need to be clarified?
- Are there any ethical considerations that are being overlooked?
- What idea(s) do you have to further strengthen the story's overarching message?

Create Social Media Stories

Whether they realize it or not, most students regularly engage in storytelling through the content they post on social media. Conveying a message on social media can be a simple yet worthwhile way to create awareness about and mobilize action around pressing social justice issues. As an educator, social media can be an effective way to engage students in storytelling using a medium with which they already feel comfortable. And

fortunately for educators, the language and structure of social media provides a scaffolded approach for story creation.

Let's pretend students in your class are creating stories to raise awareness about a social or environmental issue. Using the structure of social media to scaffold the story creation process, you could instruct students to start by coming up with a hashtag that captures the message they want to convey to the public. Once they develop a hashtag, they should write a concise message (i.e., a tweet) about their topic in 280 characters or less. Finally, students can construct a more detailed social media story about their topic using a photo and caption or a video.

#HaikuYourStory

This simple activity is a fun and easy way to get students thinking about how they can concisely convey the core message of their story through the creation of a haiku—a short, unrhymed form poem with Japanese origins. The haiku is characterized by three lines which follow a five-seven-five syllable pattern: five syllables in the first line, seven syllables in the second line, and five in the third. The beauty of the haiku is in its simplicity, so students shouldn't overthink this activity. Students can decide whether they want to title their haiku, though one or two words should be sufficient.

> **Teaching Tip:**
>
> If you teach STEM, consider asking students to create a sciku or scientific haiku, a term coined by The Sciku Project. Scikus nurture creativity while affording students the opportunity to think and write about complex scientific issues in ways a lay audience can understand.

Below is an example, written by Maru Gonzalez, one of the book's authors.

> Minds open, hearts change,
> Blurring the dividing line.
> Stories connect us.

Concluding Thoughts

Building a story can seem like an intimidating endeavor. The practices we've reviewed in this chapter are intended to help students generate ideas that will inform and shape intentional, reflective, and ethically grounded stories. You can support students by offering specific, meaningful, and instructive feedback and providing resources to facilitate the story creation process. Next up, we'll examine how students can broaden the scope of their message and drive individual and collective action.

Questions for Extended Student Dialogue

- Which of these practices did you find most helpful?
- What resources or support do you still need?
- Why is reflection an important part of the story building process?
- How has giving and receiving feedback improved your story?

Questions to Encourage Educator Self-Reflection

- How have these practices improved students' stories?
- Where are students struggling? How can you best support them?

- Pay attention to group dynamics. Which students are participating? Which students, if any, seem less engaged?
- In what ways can you assist students in the process of feedback and peer review?

References

COMPASS Science Communication. (2023). *The Message Box.* COMPASS.

Gonzalez, M., Kokozos, M., Nyota, N., & Byrd, C. (2023). Youth storytelling for social change: Guiding questions for effective and ethical delivery. *Journal of Extension*, *61*(3). doi:10.34068/joe.61.03.03

11

Beyond the Story

Moving from Awareness to Critical Action

As part of his involvement with the youth council, Max is accustomed to thinking about and engaging in issues and initiatives impacting his local community. From coordinating the annual holiday food drive to serving on the advisory committee for his town's new community center, Max has always been first in line to lend a hand.

Soon after the start of junior year, though, his once sunny demeanor grew somber, burdened by the weight of expectations and mounting obligations. With each passing day, Max was losing confidence in his ability to successfully balance school, friends, extracurriculars, college applications, and a new part-time job while trying to maintain his reputation as a leader and model student. He felt overwhelmed, exhausted, and anxious. His days were consumed by stress and anxiety, bookended by early mornings and late-night study sessions. Rinse, repeat.

Never the type to ask for help, Max kept pushing through.

Until he couldn't.

As isolated as Max felt, he wasn't alone. He could sense a discernible rise in anxiety, disconnection, and depression among

his peers. And, yet, no one was talking about it; the silence was almost palpable.

So he decided to speak up.

At the next youth council meeting, Max opened up about his growing feelings of anxiety and disconnection. He shared his struggle to navigate escalating pressures and expectations. And he disclosed the shame he felt asking for help, especially as a male. Max also connected his experience to a broader reality facing young people both in his community and across the country, citing documented increases of anxiety, depression, and suicide among youth. Finally, Max called for more dialogue, resources, and understanding—not just in response to his experience but for the countless young people who are struggling in silence.

Max's story was received with empathy. Max's words resonated with and validated those who saw their challenges reflected in his story. Even those who couldn't directly understand Max's experience gained a new awareness of mental health and how they might contribute to a culture of compassion, support, and wellness.

Yet, as inspiring as his story was, Max knew he had more work to do. He felt a growing responsibility to advocate for mental health awareness, resources, and education. As outlined in our guiding principles, Max understood that *stories aren't the end; they're the starting point*. For Max, his story was a gateway for mobilizing critical action and creating sustainable, systemic change, including a collective commitment to actively address the stigma that surrounds mental health.

Throughout this book, we've witnessed countless examples of students harnessing their stories to effectively raise public consciousness about the most pressing social issues of our time—from environmental justice, racial equity, and disability awareness to LGBTQIA+ rights and homelessness, among other topics. This chapter shifts the focus from awareness to critical action. We follow Max's advocacy journey while highlighting the knowledge and skills needed to help students broaden the scope of their message, identify and leverage their

strengths, and establish coalitions to drive individual and collective action.

From "Story of Self" to "Story of Now"

As Max's story illustrates, raising awareness is often the first step, but social change requires moving beyond our individual stories and into collective action. To that end, let's revisit and expand what we've learned about the public narrative (Ganz, 2011), an iterative leadership practice that links an individual's story (a story of self) to the shared goals and values of a community (a story of us), translating them into a call for mobilization and coalition building in service of a shared purpose (a story of now).

Let's revisit Max. His "story of us" might be the shared experience of stress and anxiety among his peers and young people in general, their common desire for a more supportive school environment, and their belief that everyone deserves access to mental health resources. This story reveals shared values and a common purpose: improving youth mental health. As illustrated in Max's story, identifying commonality helped foster a sense of belonging, solidarity, and collective power, reminding listeners they are not alone in struggle, and that together change is possible.

Next, let's zoom in on Max's "story of now." His anxiety, for example, and his courageous decision to speak up about it, shines a light on a pressing issue affecting countless young people today: the youth mental health crisis. Max's "story of self" coupled with his "story of us," translates into his "story of now." It's a story unfolding in the present moment, shaped by the complex interplay of individual experiences and societal forces. By recognizing the urgency of this challenge and its connection to the various layers of his social environment, Max can begin to identify potential pathways for individual and collective action.

The "story of now" helps bridge the gap between personal and collective stories and social change; it allows students to

connect their experiences to the larger issues affecting their communities and the world and call the audience to action. By understanding how their stories fit into a broader narrative, students gain a deeper understanding of the challenges they will face and identify opportunities for collective action. That's the focus of this chapter—the *what now* and *what's next*. Whether students have built a public narrative or tackled a different storytelling format, these questions—the ones that shape the story of now—will help move students from awareness to critical action.

The Interconnection of Our Stories

Just as Max's story resonated with his peers and sparked a collective desire for change, our individual stories are often deeply interconnected and contribute to a larger narrative of social transformation. This interconnectedness manifests in two important ways.

First, readers and listeners often connect with our stories, sometimes even seeing themselves reflected in them. When Max bravely disclosed his struggles with anxiety, he gave voice to the silent struggles of his classmates who were facing similar challenges. This realization—that we are not alone in our experiences—can be incredibly empowering; it fosters a sense of belonging, solidarity, and shared purpose, laying the groundwork for collective action. Research in social psychology has shown that this sense of shared identity is a powerful motivator for social change, as it reinforces our commitment to a cause and increases our willingness to act (van Zomeren et al., 2008).

Second, even when our stories appear different on the surface, they often share common threads, particularly when it comes to the roots of oppression and injustice. For instance, while Max's story focuses on mental health, it also touches upon issues of gender norms and pressures to succeed. These underlying themes may resonate with students facing societal expectations and assumptions related to their race, ethnicity, sexual orientation, or socioeconomic status, among other identities.

Activity Spotlight: Connecting the Dots

In this activity, students will identify potential connections between their story's topic (e.g., gun violence, foster care reform, school funding) and those of their peers. Before facilitating this activity, think about how students' topics are connected; be ready to provide examples or prompting for students who may feel stuck. For example, you could note that a student focused on accessible healthcare might draw a line linking their topic to mental health and wellness or that a student focused on environmental justice could connect their issue to food waste and fast fashion.

- On a whiteboard or piece of chart paper, write down the overarching topic driving each students' story (e.g., accessible healthcare, mental health and wellness, bullying prevention). Be sure to leave space between the topics.
- Ask students to think about what topic(s) overlap with or connect to theirs.
- Next, ask students to draw a line(s) between their topic and the one(s) where there is overlap. Depending on the size of the group, consider asking each student to use a different colored marker.
- By the end of the activity, students will have produced a web of connections. Go through each of the connections, asking which topics overlap and in what ways.
- Follow up by asking how students might work across issues toward a shared goal, what they might gain from collaboration, and how they can ensure reciprocity. Students may observe that all their topics ultimately overlap, presenting an opportunity to highlight the interconnectedness of social justice issues.

Taking it a step further, Max might identify and work to address the ways in which poverty, racism, transphobia, and other manifestations of oppression exacerbate mental health issues like anxiety, depression, and suicidal ideation, and create barriers to access adequate and affordable care. Recognizing these shared roots can create powerful alliances across different social movements, as students from diverse backgrounds unite to challenge the systems that perpetuate inequity.

By understanding the interconnectedness of stories, students can move beyond individual struggles and tap into their collective power for change. For example, a student noticing that some classmates struggle with online learning due to lack of internet access or outdated technology might uncover the digital divide, where unequal access to technology reinforces existing inequalities in education and opportunities. Another student hearing harmful stereotypes about immigrants might examine the complexities of immigration policies and the challenges faced by immigrant communities due to prejudice and misinformation. These realizations, alongside understanding that mental health challenges often reflect societal pressures and stigma, ignite a sense of responsibility and agency. Students become motivated to join forces with others and take critical action. Instead of feeling alone, they become empowered to address the root causes of these issues, advocating for things like school-provided technology, challenging harmful stereotypes, and better mental health services.

Toward Critical Action

To be critical, action should be informed and reflective; it should aim to drive social change that is equitable, sustainable, and systemic (Watts et al., 2011). Whether in research or practice, we have found that students who engage in social impact storytelling are more likely to participate in or commit to taking critical action, both individually and collaboratively (Gonzalez et al., 2024). But what might critical action look like in practice? What does it *not* look like? In the case of Max, an example of a *non*-critical action

might be advocating for a mindfulness workshop for students. Such an effort, while potentially effective in the short term, likely won't generate sustainable, systemic change. In contrast, critically grounded action would be guided by questions like: What policies, practices, and conditions exacerbate student mental health struggles and keep them from speaking openly about their mental health needs? What must happen—individually, collectively, and institutionally—to change said policies, practices, and conditions such that student mental health improves in the long term? With whom can we collaborate?

Of course, there is no one right way to engage in critical action. As mentioned in Chapter 1, not all social change agents are on the frontlines of a protest march chanting into a megaphone or meeting with legislators to change policy; most are working behind the scenes in a variety of roles. Indeed, some students, particularly those who are more reserved and introverted, may struggle to view themselves as effective mobilizers and change agents. Beyond reiterating the various pathways of engagement, consider asking students to take stock of their strengths and skills, particularly as they relate to teamwork. Then, ask them how they might leverage their strengths and skills, both individually and collaboratively. For example, a student who describes themselves as detail-oriented, tech savvy, organized, and caring may decide to broaden their message through digital mediums like podcasts and social media platforms. As a member of a team, that same student could apply her strengths by taking meeting notes, managing a budget, and regularly checking in with team members to ensure well-being.

 Teaching Tip:

To help students think more broadly about applying their strengths and skills to drive action, check out Iyer's (2017) Social Change Ecosystem Map. This framework details ten roles—weavers, experimenters, frontline responders, visionaries, builders, caregivers, disrupters, healers,

> storytellers, and guides—individuals can play in promoting social change. Complementary resources are available to download online and can help students think about how they can effectively harness their strengths, values, and interests to collaborate for social change.

Identifying Spheres of Influence

Before confirming *how* they want to move from awareness to critical action, students should take stock of who they know and what resources they can leverage to maximize their impact. The Spheres of Influence model (Zúñiga, 2020), illustrated and adapted in Figure 11.1, is a useful tool for identifying where and with whom students can expand their reach. The innermost circle focuses on the self and calls on students to think about how they can continue learning about their issue to become more informed and effective messengers. The second sphere consists of students' close family and friends, those with whom they have the greatest influence. The third sphere is made up of social, school, and extracurricular networks, which include the people with whom a student regularly interacts such as neighbors, acquaintances, friends, teammates, and classmates. The fourth sphere is the community and is characterized by community organizations, local elected officials, and individuals with whom students interact less frequently. Given the role of social media, we added a fifth sphere to this model, the digital sphere, which consists of students' social media presence and networks.

Let's revisit Max and explore his potential spheres of influence. Starting with the innermost sphere, Max could educate himself by conducting further research on the youth mental health crisis or following social media accounts focused on educating the public about this issue. In the second sphere, Max may decide to have conversations with his parents and close friends, encouraging them to learn more and take action. For the social, schools, and work relationships sphere, Max has already

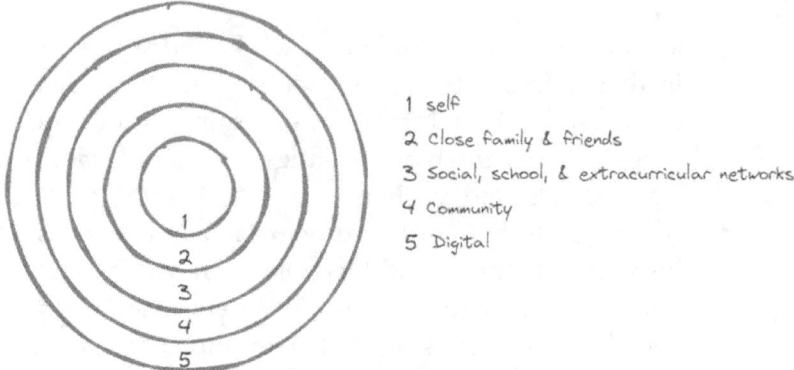

FIGURE 11.1 SPHERES OF INFLUENCE MODEL VISUALIZATION
Source: Informed by the work of Zúñiga (2020)

addressed members of his youth council. He could go a step further and work with his school community to create a task force focused on student mental health. In the community sphere, Max can identify and collaborate with local wellness organizations; likewise, he could address and work with the local school board on district-wide student mental health initiatives. Finally, within the digital sphere, Max can think about how to expand his message through his social media channels.

 Activity Spotlight: Identifying Spheres of Influence

In this activity, students will identify their spheres of influence. Before beginning, consider walking students through each sphere of the model and provide examples like the ones illustrated in Figure 11.1.

- **Self:** First, ask students to turn their focus inward: What do they still have left to learn about the issue they seek to address? What steps will they take to deepen their knowledge and build the skills needed to broaden their impact?
- **Close family and friends:** Next, ask students to make a list of the people closest to them like immedi-

ate family members and best friends, and structures in their microsystem, those with whom they have daily face-to-face interactions. Examples include parents and caregivers, siblings, mentors, school, close friends, and teachers.
- **Social, school, and extracurricular networks:** Instruct students to add people with whom they interact on a regular basis like peers, teammates, neighbors, and classmates. For example, a student passionate about environmental justice could collaborate with their school's environmental club to organize a recycling initiative or partner with a local youth organization to host a community cleanup day.
- **Community:** Here, students should include community organizations, after-school programs, and elected officials—people and structures that are less proximal to students' daily functioning but with whom and where they can still have influence. For instance, a student interested in creating sensory-friendly classrooms may meet with administrators to advocate for professional development for teachers.
- **Digital:** For this sphere, ask students to focus specifically on social media, citing its growing role in informing culture. Students should think about their online presence: What social media platforms are they active on? What people or organizations are they connected to?

Collaboration: Amplifying Impact Through Collective Action

Collaboration is often key to achieving lasting social change (Haushalter & Steinberg, 2024). When executed effectively, collaboration involves working with people who share a common vision, bringing together diverse perspectives and skills, and

pooling resources to amplify impact (Bryson et al., 2015). To that end, social impact storytelling can play a vital role in fostering collaboration. For example, during the Labor Movement, stories of harsh working conditions, low wages, and worker exploitation, shared through union publications, songs, and oral histories, helped to unite workers and build solidarity in their fight for fair labor practices (Foner, 2022). Similarly, the Disability Rights Movement gained strength as individuals shared their experiences of discrimination and exclusion, leading to the passage of landmark legislation like the Americans with Disabilities Act (Davis, 2016). And today, youth-led climate activism utilizes social media platforms to share personal narratives of experiencing climate change impacts, fostering collaboration among diverse groups worldwide and mobilizing them toward a shared vision of a sustainable future (Goldman, 2022).

Collaboration requires a set of skills and strategies that can be learned and practiced. First and foremost, building strong relationships is essential. This involves active listening, empathy, and a genuine interest in understanding the perspectives and needs of potential collaborators (Bastien & Holmarsdottir, 2017). Start by encouraging students to seek out and partner with individuals and organizations representing the communities most affected by the issues they are addressing and engage in dialogue with them in a respectful manner. But don't just tell students to collaborate—show them how! Model the initial steps of contacting a potential partner. This could involve drafting an email, role-playing a phone call, and facilitating a class discussion on different ways to initiate collaboration, such as using social media, attending events, or leveraging existing connections.

 Activity Spotlight: Collaborating for Change

Divide students into small groups (e.g., 3 to 4). Ask them to identify one issue impacting their school or community or assign an issue. Examples include mental health, food waste, and bullying, among many others. Next, ask students to

imagine they are part of a newly established youth-led task force aimed at addressing the identified or assigned issue. Students should think about how they can leverage their collective strengths, interests, networks, and storytelling skills to identify the task force's values and develop a core message and detailed action plan using the following questions to guide their decisions:

- What is our overarching message and how and with whom can we communicate it? Refer to Chapter 10 for impact-driven storybuilding resources.
- How can we ensure our actions are informed?
  - What does the research say about our issue?
  - What are the needs of the population affected by this issue?
  - What resources already exist within our school and/or community?
- Who are our potential partners?
- What steps will we take to prioritize the needs and voices of the people most affected by this issue?
- What steps can be taken to ensure everyone on the task force contributes?

Once finished, students should present their task force's work to the larger group. Work with them to debrief the activity, ask questions, and identify patterns across each group's collaborative process.

Community Partnerships: Expanding the Circle of Support

Forming partnerships with community organizations, local leaders, and other stakeholders offers invaluable opportunities for students to take their learning beyond the classroom. These partnerships provide real-world experience, allowing students to gain firsthand knowledge and develop practical skills while deepening their understanding of social justice issues (Haushalter & Steinberg, 2024). Community partners also bring a wealth of

experience to the table; they serve as mentors and role models, providing guidance, support, and inspiration to students as they navigate their advocacy journeys. Furthermore, partnerships can provide access to resources that may not be available within the school or community setting, such as funding, expertise, and networks, which can significantly enhance the impact and sustainability of student-led initiatives.

Imagine a high school class studying environmental justice. By partnering with a local conservation organization, students can gain hands-on experience conducting water quality testing in their community. This collaboration could lead to advocacy efforts to address pollution concerns, empowering students to make a tangible difference in their local environment. Similarly, a student group focused on food insecurity could collaborate with a local food bank to organize a food drive and raise awareness about hunger in their community. These real-world experiences not only provide valuable learning opportunities but also demonstrate how collaboration can expand our circle of support and contribute to meaningful change.

Activity Spotlight: Community Mapping—Expanding Your Reach

To effectively collaborate with community partners and leverage those resources, students need a clear understanding of the landscape of support available to them. This activity guides students to visually map their spheres of influence (Zúñiga, 2020), identifying key collaborators and resources within their community and beyond. Using a digital mapping tool like Google Maps (or an alternative), students chart their potential reach from the classroom to the (digital) world, uncovering a network of potential allies. Before beginning this activity, consider demonstrating how to use the chosen mapping tool and provide examples of how to categorize and connect different types of resources.

- ♦ First, ask students to drop a pin on the map to represent their school or the location of their community-

based program. They should then populate this immediate environment—their microsystem—with classmates, teachers, and relevant school resources (e.g., library, after-school clubs).
- Next, instruct students to expand their search outward, adding locations within a 1-mile radius of their school. Encourage them to identify community organizations, libraries, community centers, and other resources that might be relevant to their chosen cause.
- Now, broaden the scope to a 5- to 20-mile radius, encompassing suburban and/or city-level resources. This may include government offices, larger non-profits, businesses, and media outlets that could play a role in advancing their goals.
- Explain that the 20- to 50-mile radius (and beyond) represents the regional landscape. Here, students can pinpoint universities, specialized service providers, advocacy groups, and other resources that may offer expertise or support.
- Finally, introduce the concept of "infinity"—the digital sphere. This is where students can map online resources, social media groups, national organizations, and global movements related to their cause.

As students populate their maps, remind them to:

- **categorize** entries using different colors or icons (e.g., educational, political, social)
- **research** each entry to gather basic information (contact, mission, etc.)
- **connect** related entries to visualize potential partnerships.

Once they're done, ask students:

- What surprised you about the resources available in your community?

- Did you discover any potential partners you weren't aware of before?
- How can this map help you act on the issue you care about?
- What are the benefits and challenges of collaborating with organizations at different levels (local, regional, national, online)?

This activity allows students to visualize their network of support, strategically plan their outreach efforts, and recognize the broad and diverse range of collaborators who can help them make a difference.

Navigating and Sustaining Partnerships

As students begin to engage with community partners and expand their collaborative efforts, it's essential to equip them with the skills to navigate diverse perspectives and social boundaries. Haushalter and Steinberg (2024) highlight the importance of "boundary spanning"—the ability to effectively navigate these social boundaries to foster collaboration and achieve shared goals. This involves understanding and respecting different forms of knowledge, adapting to diverse communication styles, and building relationships with individuals from various backgrounds. For instance, a student advocating for environmental justice might need to collaborate with scientists, community activists, policymakers, and business leaders, each with their own perspectives and priorities.

By embracing a "developmental mindset" (Haushalter & Steinberg, 2024), students can approach these collaborations with openness, humility, and a willingness to learn and adapt, ultimately enhancing their ability to partner with others. Beyond building relationships, effective collaboration also requires clear and respectful communication. This includes expressing ideas clearly, actively listening to others, and being open to different viewpoints. It's also crucial to establish shared goals and a

common understanding of the problem and potential solutions. By fostering a culture of open communication and mutual respect, students can navigate disagreements constructively and work together more effectively toward their shared vision. Moreover, maintaining these partnerships requires careful planning and ongoing communication. Students should be encouraged to consider the "life cycle of collaboration," starting with small-scale pilot projects and gradually expanding as trust and shared understanding develop (Haushalter & Steinberg, 2024). Strong communication channels and accountability mechanisms are essential to ensure all partners are informed and engaged.

Implementation and Evaluation: A Continuous Cycle

Moving from awareness to critical action requires not only developing an action plan but also implementing and evaluating it effectively. This process is not linear; it's a continuous cycle of planning, action, reflection, and adjustment. Encourage students to break down their action plans into smaller, manageable steps, providing support and guidance as they navigate challenges and celebrate their successes along the way. Help students develop strategies for measuring the impact of their actions. This might involve collecting data, gathering feedback, or assessing progress toward their goals. Encourage students to reflect on their experiences, both successes and challenges, and consider what lessons they have learned and how they can apply those lessons to future actions. Based on their reflections and evaluations, help students adjust their action plans as needed. This iterative process enables flexibility and continuous improvement.

Take a student named Johnny, for example, who learns about the disproportionate impact of air pollution on low-income communities of color. He decides to take action. First, he researches the sources of pollution in his city and identifies a nearby factory emitting harmful pollutants. Next, he joins a local environmental justice organization and participates in community meetings to learn about the concerns of residents and existing efforts to address the issue. Johnny then helps organize a petition and a community rally to raise awareness and demand stricter emission controls

on the factory. After these initial actions, Johnny reflects on their effectiveness. Did the rally attract media attention? Did the petition lead to policy changes? Based on his reflections, Johnny might adjust the action plan, perhaps focusing on lobbying city council members or partnering with other community groups to amplify their voices. Throughout this process, Johnny continually evaluates the impact of his actions by tracking air quality data, collecting resident testimonials, and monitoring policy developments. This iterative process of planning, action, reflection, and adjustment allows Johnny to be flexible and adapt his strategies to achieve meaningful and sustainable change in the fight for environmental justice.

Gratitude and Appreciation: Celebrating Storytellers and Supporters

In the midst of advocating for change, it's important to pause and express gratitude for the individuals who have shared their stories and supported the process. Encourage students to celebrate each other, acknowledging and appreciating the courage and vulnerability it takes to share personal narratives. Create opportunities for students to thank each other for their contributions and celebrate their collective efforts. Also, encourage students to express their appreciation to the mentors, educators, family members, and community members who have supported their journey. Such an exchange fosters a sense of community and strengthens relationships, creating a supportive network for continued growth and action. Some specific ideas for celebration include peer-to-peer shout-outs, thank-you notes, an appreciation wall, a community gratitude board (i.e., dedicate a bulletin board to expressing gratitude to community partners, showcasing their contributions), and hosting a small party, or an end-of-the-year showcase.

Putting It All Together: From Story to Action

Building upon the foundation of collaboration, the journey from awareness to critical action requires a roadmap—an action plan. This plan will be the vehicle that carries students' stories and

aspirations forward, transforming their understanding of social issues into tangible steps toward change. Before they begin developing this plan, however, it's crucial for them to synthesize the key concepts and skills they've learned throughout this chapter. Encourage them to reflect on the following questions:

- How has your understanding of the public narrative evolved? How can you use the "story of self," "story of us," and "story of now" framework to connect your personal experiences to broader social issues and inspire collective action?
- How can you build strong collaborative relationships?
- How can you identify and connect with potential collaborators within your spheres of influence? What resources and support can you access through community partnerships?
- How can you develop an action plan that is informed, strategic, and aligned with your values and goals?
- How can you implement and evaluate your action plan effectively, ensuring that it is sustainable and leads to meaningful change?
- How can you express gratitude and appreciation to those who have supported your journey and contributed to your efforts?

By reflecting on these questions, students can synthesize their learning and prepare to take action on the issues they care about.

 Activity Spotlight: Building an Action Plan

Now that students have a firm grasp of the foundational concepts, they can begin building their action plans, a process that requires intentionality and goal setting. Building an action plan will help students identify next steps and reflect on what they need to be successful. Students should

complete this activity individually, guided by the following prompts:

- **Identifying the Challenge:** What is the most urgent challenge related to your issue that demands action now? What measurable steps will you take to address this challenge? What support and resources do you still need?
- **Defining Your Role:** What role do you want to play in calling for action? How will you leverage your strengths and skills?
- **Broadening Your Reach:** How will you broaden the reach of your story with the people, institutions, and organizations that make up your spheres of influence? What role will social media play?
- **Collaborating for Change:** What people and organizations will you collaborate with to expand your message? How might people and organizations across your spheres of influence connect and collaborate to drive collective action?
- **Measuring Impact:** How will you measure your impact? What indicators will show that your actions are making a difference?

Concluding Thoughts

The transition from awareness to critical action is not always easy, but it is a worthwhile journey, filled with hope and possibility. As we have seen in this chapter, when students understand their spheres of influence, pursue collaboration, and leverage their additional unique strengths, they can transform their stories into catalysts for change.

Students' voices matter.

Their actions have an impact.

And together, they can build a more just and equitable world.

Now, it's your turn.

Whether you teach in a classroom or a youth-serving organization, take that first step to amplify students' voices.

We need their stories more than ever.

> **Questions for Extended Student Dialogue**
>
> - What are some examples of critical action that young people are taking to address social challenges in your community or the world?
> - How can you identify and leverage your strengths and skills to take critical action on an issue you care about?
> - Why is collaboration important for achieving social change, and how can you effectively collaborate with others?
> - What are some potential obstacles you might encounter when trying to create change, and how can you overcome them?
> - How can storytelling be used to inspire and mobilize others for positive change?

> **Questions to Encourage Educator Self-Reflection**
>
> - How can you create a classroom environment that encourages students to move from awareness to critical action?
> - What are some ways you can help students connect their personal stories to broader social issues and public narratives?
> - How can you support students in developing the skills and confidence they need to become effective change agents?

- How can you support students in navigating potential pushback or resistance to their advocacy efforts?
- How can you help students develop a sense of hope and agency, even when faced with complex and seemingly intractable social problems?
- What resources or tools can you provide to help students identify and connect with potential collaborators in their community?
- How can you integrate critical action projects into your curriculum to provide students with authentic opportunities to make a difference?
- How can you use storytelling to model critical engagement and inspire students to become active participants in shaping their world?

References

Bastien, S., & Holmarsdottir, H. B. (2017). *Youth as architects of social change: Global efforts to advance youth-driven innovation*. Springer International Publishing.

Bryson, J. M., Crosby, B. C., & Stone, M. M. (2015). *Collaboration: A strategic guide to navigating complex terrain* (2nd ed.). Jossey-Bass.

Davis, L. J. (2016). *Enabling acts: The hidden story of how the Americans with Disabilities Act gave the largest US minority its rights*. Beacon Press.

Foner, P. S. (2022). *History of the labor movement in the United States, Vol. 1: From colonial times to the founding of the American Federation of Labor*. International Publishers.

Ganz, M. (2011). Public narrative, collective action, and power. In S. Odugbemi & T. Lee (Eds.), *Accountability through public opinion: From inertia to public action* (pp. 273–289). The World Bank.

Goldman, L. (2022). *Climate change and youth: Turning grief and anxiety into activism* (1st ed.). Routledge.

Gonzalez, M., Kokozos, M., McKee, K., & Byrd, C. (2024). Storytelling through a Critical Positive Youth Development framework: A mixed

methods approach. *Journal of Youth Development*, *19*(1). https://tigerprints.clemson.edu/jyd/vol19/iss1/2

Haushalter, K., & Steinberg, P. (2024, May 2). Collaboration across social boundaries: A practical guide. *Stanford Social Innovation Review*. https://ssir.org/articles/entry/collaboration-across-social-boundaries#

Iyer, D. (2017). *The social change map*. The Social Change Map. https://socialchangemap.com/home/understanding-the-framework

van Zomeren, M., Postmes, T., & Spears, R. (2008). Toward an integrative social identity model of collective action: A quantitative research synthesis of three socio-psychological perspectives. *Psychological Bulletin*, *134*(4), 504–535. https://doi.org/10.1037/0033-2909.134.4.504

Watts, R. J., Diemer, M. A., & Voight, A. M. (2011). Critical consciousness: Current status & future directions. *New Directions for Child & Adolescent Development*, *2011*(134), 43–57. doi:10.1002/cd.310

Zúñiga, X. (2020). *EDUC 202: Exploring issues in intergroup dialogue curricular guide*. Social Justice Education, University of Massachusetts Amherst.

Afterword

Austin Laufersweiler

As you've learned, the immediate benefits of youth-led storytelling are evident, both for young people and the communities they engage. But what happens long-term when students are given the opportunity, tools, and platform to share their stories? How are they transformed when their ideas, insights, and experiences are heard, valued, and solicited?

While I can't speak for all students, I can share my story.

Let's go back to 2007. I was a sophomore in high school and had just come out as gay. I remember telling my family that I planned to be discreet about my identity, with no intention to make my sexual orientation a defining part of my life. I even vowed to forgo marriage at the risk of making a political statement.

I grew up in what was, at the time, the most conservative county in the country (times have changed, and now my hometown of Marietta, Georgia is a more vibrant and inclusive place). I felt extremely isolated in a high school with very little demographic diversity, and because I was not accepted for my queerness at home, I became noticeably distracted at school.

It's when I was called into the school social worker's office to discuss my home life that I noticed a rainbow sticker on a school counselor's door. That moment changed the trajectory of my high school experience, and the rest of my life.

The counseling staff at my high school provided me with a safe space. They connected me with opportunities to make a difference through peer helper organizations and tutoring programs, and I began to feel a greater sense of confidence and belonging. When I decided I was ready to start our school's gender and sexuality alliance, the counseling staff stood behind me despite firm opposition from the school's leadership.

I was finding my voice at the same time that instances of bullying against LGBTQIA+ students in Georgia started making the local news. Some of my school's counseling staff had planned to attend our county's school board meeting to share the importance of inclusive anti-bullying policies. I didn't know the first thing about advocacy and I had severe doubts that anyone would take me seriously. Still, the counseling staff encouraged me to join them, speak about my experience at school and how improved policies could protect students from bullying and administrators from unwanted controversy.

As a high school student, I didn't have a firm grasp on the intricacies of policy nor how it could affect my day-to-day experience. The educators by my side could have handed me a script and instructed me how to make my case. But that's not the approach they chose, and it made all the difference for my own development and the trust I gained in them.

They shared with me model bullying policies, explained the pros and cons of different approaches, and what factors might go into school board members' decisions. Equipped with the necessary information, I made up my own mind about what I believed and how I wanted to present my thoughts. I felt in control—like I had been provided with the information and tools to make my argument effectively.

When I faltered, they led with support and encouragement. They gave me the space to ask for advice and suggestions to improve my argument. I never felt the power imbalance in our relationship. I was treated as a partner, if not a leader, in our efforts.

After three school board meetings and numerous other conversations with school and county personnel, the board voted to approve a new anti-bullying policy with enumerated categories inclusive of LGBTQIA+ students and others across a host of demographic categories. The policy was also adopted as the model policy for the state of Georgia—a major win for safe schools across the state.

The experience had transformed me. I felt the power of my voice and I saw what an impact I could make. Those educators changed my life, and continued to by connecting me with national organizations that would help me grow my impact. I would go on to lobby Congress and attend an event at the White House, where I met federal policymakers interested in our work. I also shared my story with educators and the local media to advocate for research-based practices for fostering LGBTQIA+ inclusion in schools and communities.

In 2007, I was a shy high school student afraid of his own voice and unaware of his potential. By learning to share my story, I became a confident advocate—changing policy, helping students across the state feel safer at school and giving educators the knowledge and skills to transform their schools and classrooms. Later in life, I would become the first openly gay student body president at the University of Georgia, move to Washington, DC and have a fulfilling career in the US Congress and on political campaigns. It was possible for me because I had educators in my corner who gave me the tools to effectively and ethically use my voice for social impact while treating me with dignity, compassion, and respect. They cared about the causes we all believed in, but in all our work together, they prioritized my psychological safety, development, and empowerment.

By embracing the lessons of this book, you are gaining the tools to change lives. I know this because one of the book's authors, Dr. Maru Gonzalez, was among the educators who profoundly changed my life in ways that continue to resonate well into adulthood.

Now it's your turn to take what you've learned in this book and apply it to your work with young people. If my story is any indication, your impact on students will be immense and the world will be a more just and compassionate place because of your dedication to and unyielding belief in the power of youth voice.

Austin Laufersweiler is a public affairs specialist based in Washington, DC. Austin grew up in Marietta, Georgia, and was selected by GLSEN as the organization's first Student Advocate of the Year when he was in high school. He attended the University of Georgia where he earned degrees in political science and communications studies, and was elected president of the student body. In the decade since he graduated college, Austin has served as a spokesperson on political campaigns, led media relations work for national non-profits and issue advocacy campaigns, and advised Members of Congress to help them navigate complex communications challenges.

Austin with author Maru Gonzalez at the White House Pride Reception in 2010

For Product Safety Concerns and Information please contact our EU representative GPSR@taylorandfrancis.com
Taylor & Francis Verlag GmbH, Kaufingerstraße 24, 80331 München, Germany

www.ingramcontent.com/pod-product-compliance
Lightning Source LLC
Chambersburg PA
CBHW070800230426
43665CB00017B/2436